W9-AUG-834

Canada: Europe's Last Chance

Claude Julien

CANADA: EUROPE'S LAST CHANCE

translated from the French by
Penny Williams

with introduction by
Blair Fraser

1968
St. Martin's Press
New York

Originally published in French as *Le Canada: dernière chance de l'Europe* by Editions Bernard Grasset, Paris; © Editions Bernard Grasset, 1965.

Library of Congress Catalogue Card No. 68-18335

Printed in Canada by McCorquodale and Blades Printers Limited for The Macmillan Company of Canada Limited 70 Bond Street, Toronto

Contents

Maps, Tables, and Graphs

Introduction

When Claude Julien's book first appeared in Paris in late 1965 it caused an immediate sensation, at least among the Canadians in France if not among the Europeans to whom it was primarily addressed. The theme, stated in the title, was an arresting thought – that Canada is a cultural, economic, and political bridgehead for Europe on the western shore of the Atlantic, and that if this bridgehead were lost the precarious equilibrium between Europe and the United States of America would be utterly destroyed and American domination of the Atlantic Community complete. This was the basis for his appeal, to Europeans in general but to Frenchmen in particular, for more interest in Canada and specifically for more investment by Europeans to offset the ever-growing fraction of American ownership in the Canadian economy.

To what extent has Claude Julien's thesis been proved and to what extent weakened by the events that have taken place in Canada since 1965?

Some of them, quite obviously, he did not foresee any more than the rest of us did, and of these the most notable was the unexpected defeat of Jean Lesage's Liberal government and the return of the Union Nationale to power in June 1966. Like most Canadians, he believed (rightly) that the Quiet Revolution in Quebec is a permanent, irreversible change of attitude on a wide range of fundamental issues, and he therefore inferred (wrongly, as things have turned out) that the government under which the Quiet Revolution began would survive for an indefinite future. Both these opinions were part of the conventional wisdom in both English and French Canada and in both the major political parties of Quebec, until the election returns on the night of June 5, 1966, were actually in. (Ex-Premier Jean Lesage couldn't believe them that night, nor for several days thereafter!)

But this slight misapprehension has proved to be quite unimportant – less important, indeed, than Claude Julien himself might have supposed when he was writing his book in 1965 – to the proposition he was trying to establish. If anything his thesis is stronger, not weaker, today than when it was first set forth. It has been, if not confirmed, at least made more plausible by the main stream of events in Canada.

We have seen, for one thing, a steady growth of self-awareness in the province of Quebec and in French Canada from coast to coast, a growth that began with the death of Maurice Duplessis in 1959 and was not stopped (contrary to some people's expectation) by the Union Nationale victory of 1966. It is true that such Quiet Revolutionaries as Paul Gérin-Lajoie, the minister of education in the Lesage Cabinet, somewhat outran public opinion with the expensive changes they introduced. The secularization of Quebec schools has been slowed, and public support for the traditional, clerical *collèges classiques* restored or reaffirmed. Redistribution of electoral districts to correct the preposterous advantage of the rural voter in Quebec, a project the Liberals unwisely failed to push through to a conclusion while they were in power, has now been indefinitely postponed by a Union Nationale which still, as always, finds its most reliable support in rural areas. But despite these defeats for the progressive and victories for the reactionary spirit in Quebec, the mood of self-assertion has persisted.

So has the mood of accommodation in English Canada. There have been some bursts of impatience, some occasional revivals of old-style Orange prejudice among the WASPs of east and west, but these attitudes have become more and more old-fashioned and quaint, symbols of rusticity and of old age.

Meanwhile, since Claude Julien completed his research, three provinces have made moves towards correcting the century-old grievance of French Canadians at the refusal of English-speaking provinces to grant the same educational rights to their French-speaking minorities that Quebec has always given to its English minority of twenty per cent. In New Brunswick the establishment of French as a language of instruction has gone far enough that in February 1967 a leading Acadian educationalist told me: 'We have no grievances now as French Canadians. Our only remaining grievance is that the poorer counties suffer, in our present tax system, for the advantage of the richer counties, and most French Canadians live in the poorer counties.' But even that remaining grievance has been removed by the enactment, and the endorsement at the general election of 1967, of Premier Louis Robichaud's Equal Opportunity Program, whereby the costs of education and of welfare are shared equally by all parts of New Brunswick.

Manitoba and Ontario have both proclaimed the intention of introducing, in the school year of 1968, classes in which French will be the language of instruction all the way from kindergarten to matriculation. Thus, in three of the nine English-speaking provinces, the sorest of all French-Canadian grievances will have been removed.

Three out of nine may sound a rather poor score, but the fact is that more than three-quarters of the 1.3 million French Canadians outside Quebec live in these three provinces. The continued intransigence of the other six is regrettable – it means, for example, that a French Canadian employed by a national corporation, and offered a promotion that involves transfer from Montreal to, say, Calgary or Vancouver, must still face a dilemma of the first magnitude, and choose between his own material advancement and his children's identity. Newcomers from Quebec are still treated, in these six provinces, in exactly the same way as immigrants from any other ex-enemy country.

Nevertheless, the fact that the grievance has been remedied for some three-quarters to four-fifths of all French-speaking Canadians *now* living outside Quebec, and that pressure on the other provinces has vastly increased in voltage, represents a vast stride forward towards genuine equality of French- and English-speaking Canadians throughout the land. Moreover, from the viewpoint of Claude Julien's thesis, the mere agitation for equality has had the same effect as its achievement. All of Canada today is more conscious of being a bilingual, bicultural nation – or 'two nations' – than ever before in its history. And this awareness bears a corollary awareness of our close relationship not just to Britain, but to Europe.

Another respect in which the shrewdness of Claude Julien's judgement has been borne out by events is the fluctuating status of the separatist movement, both in its own distinctive political parties and within the major parties. As he correctly discerned, it appeared to be waning in 1965 and this trend continued through 1966. Then it took a surge upward as a result of that extraordinary international incident, the De Gaulle visit of July 1967. But as the President of France becomes more and more a figure of the past, the previous trend of the separatist movement resumes.

Its most notable down-turn took place in the autumn of 1967 with the publication, first of René Lévesque's personal manifesto as a proposed resolution for a Quebec Liberal convention in October. The Lévesque resolution called for a 'sovereign' Quebec within a loose association to be called 'the Canadian Union'. This then prompted the president of the Quebec Liberal Federation, Eric Kierans, to come out with a ringing denunciation of 'separatism in all its forms' and a devastating appraisal of what, in terms of living standards and economic growth, any kind of separation would mean for Quebec.

Kierans made the issue a challenge to politically mortal combat, which Lévesque accepted. Each man promised to resign from the Liberal Party if his ideas were not accepted. At the convention, Lévesque and his followers were defeated by a crushing majority, and thereupon resigned to enter a kind of political limbo with no party affiliation at all.

Meanwhile in the Union Nationale the most nearly separatist of Daniel Johnson's ministers, Jean-Noël Tremblay of cultural affairs, had come out with a rather intemperate statement accusing Lévesque of 'shop-lifting' Tremblay's ideas. At the same time a curious document was leaked to the press. Purporting to be a study prepared for the Union Nationale election campaign of 1966, it set forth detailed plans for 'an independent Quebec within five years'.

In fact it had never been adopted as a campaign document by the Union Nationale, nor were its principal authors even members of the party. But the renewal of separatist talk, inside and outside Quebec, had the effect of rousing alarm among investors at the very moment when Quebec was encountering some difficulty in selling provincial bonds. The acting premier and minister of finance Paul Dozois thought it wise to call a press conference for the express purpose of declaring his belief that Quebec would be better off inside than outside Confederation. By no coincidence he singled out Jean-Noël Tremblay, the most notorious quasi-separatist in the Cabinet, to stand at his side and publicly declare: 'I share the opinion of my colleague.'

Meanwhile in business as well as political circles there was an outbreak of *anti*-separatist statements. This was the first time since the separatist movement began in 1960 that it had been denounced in French by French Canadians, in unequivocal terms.

The net result was that by the end of 1967 the whole 'constitutional issue' had been taken out of the hands of the legal theologians, law professors, and amateur politicians and given over to practical men of affairs who had no intention of allowing these ivory-tower dwellers to damage the Quebec economy. By the same token, however, they were more anxious than ever to attract European investment, more assiduous than ever in cultivating contacts in metropolitan France.

Thus Claude Julien's theme is even more topical today in Europe and in Canada than when it was written. Certainly the interest in Canada, which he urges so eloquently upon his countrymen, has been aroused during 1967 – not altogether in ways of which he would approve, but aroused none the less. It may or may not find expression in an increase of European investment in Canada, but in either case it provides a focus and a rationale for sentiments on both sides of the Atlantic that have previously been rather vague and diffuse, but that are genuine.

Whether or not Canada is literally 'Europe's last chance', it is certainly Europe's last foothold, last bridgehead if you will, on the North American continent. It seems reasonable to suggest that Europe could and should do more to improve this position and that the atmosphere within Canada has never been more favourable to such enterprise than it is right now.

Ottawa, November 15, 1967   *Blair Fraser*

Europe and Canada

Canada has taught me that irritation can inspire a book. Irritation at hearing an academic in a semi-official organization talk about Quebec in terms of Maria Chapdelaine, as if one of the world's largest aluminum companies were not now operating on the shores of the same Lake St. John where Louis Hémon's heroine once languished. Irritation at reading an English-Canadian professor's comments on French-Canadian attachment to 'ancient ties, an ancient faith, an ancient language' – remarks made with the patronizing condescension of an American travelling salesman visiting an Indian reservation. The irritation of discovering in the *Columbia Encyclopedia* that Quebeckers, no matter how distinguished, 'speak a French patois'. Such ignorance justifies a real concern when the Texan resident in the White House sharply reprimands the Prime Minister of Canada, recipient of a Nobel Peace Prize, for daring to express his own opinions on a policy that affects the destiny of the entire Western world.

Frankly, Canada has mismanaged its entry on the international scene. Since the Second World War its Gross National Product has increased almost tenfold, yet the rest of us only notice its existence when bombs explode in an English section of Montreal. The important role played by Canada in international affairs is too often unknown, though provocative (albeit useless) gestures would probably make a greater impression. Catholics in France, complacent about their *avant-garde* faith, look upon Quebec as a priest-ridden, reactionary society. They were amazed to see the Cardinal Archbishop of Montreal completely overshadow the most renowned French prelates at the Vatican Council. And they are still unaware that the secularization of Catholic unions took place in Canada before it did in France!

Yet this conceit has its humorous side. A French popular-science writer crossed the Atlantic to talk about nuclear research to the best atomic-energy minds at Chalk River. And an important French industrialist wrote to the mayor of Montreal, Jean Drapeau, in English.

But a Frenchman finds cause for irritation in Canada itself. A few conversations with a certain type of Anglo-Saxon will make him fervently pro-separatist. Fortunately, the antidote is very simple; a few inflamed speeches from the most narrow-minded of the nationalists, and he will suddenly feel very close to the efficient, phlegmatic 'damned English'!

The reality, of course, is much more complex, and that is why Canada, reputed to be so boring, is actually so fascinating to analyse. Its two founding races rejected the American melting-pot for an experiment in building a bilingual, bicultural society. Today they know and trust each other so little that the continued existence of this 1867 confederation pact is in doubt. How did it happen? How has Quebec managed to throw off the time-honoured rural, clerical, and traditional structures, to plunge itself into the world of big business and advanced thinking when, only ten years ago, it rejected the outside world as a source of contamination? How can English and French Canada, together or separately, avoid becoming satellites of the United States?

These questions matter to non-Canadians as well. If Canada's great economic potential were to merge with the power of the United States, equilibrium between the two sides of the Atlantic would be lost. Europe would have to bend its knee, knowing its interests would never again prevail in the Atlantic alliance. Canadians, absorbed in linguistic quarrels, forget this international dimension to their internal problem. They sit in a closed circle, lifting their heads from morose introspection only to berate Canadians who speak the other language. Turned in on themselves, they wake up periodically to discover they have fallen just a little bit more under American influence. But they soon sink back into torpor, for how can they effectively resist the American giant who daily nibbles away at their independence and their identity? And by themselves they cannot resist. But Canadians ought to realize that they are not, and cannot be, alone. Whether most Europeans are aware of the fact or not, part, and perhaps the decisive part, of the destiny of Europe is at stake in Canada. If this country of more than eighteen million people and immense natural resources becomes in any way a branch office of the United States, the Americans will no longer even pretend to treat Europe as an equal.

It is frustrating to see French and English Canadians wearing themselves out in sterile debate – sterile because it ignores the international dimension. But it is just as upsetting to see how few Europeans realize what influence Canada could have on their own future. Even if western Europe were perfectly united, it still would not balance the United States, particularly if Canada were to become virtually a part of that country. Europe must salvage what freedom of movement it can by winning all possible support in Asia, Africa, and the American continent. Canada commands a special position in this far-reaching plan because of its natural resources, its high level of industrialization, and its ancient ties with Great Britain and France. Europe will be hastening its own decline if it allows the United States to supplant it in Africa, if it looks on Latin America as the private hunting-ground of the U.S.A., or if it abandons to Washington all policy decisions on Asia. In all three areas Europe can think of Canada as a prime ally, an indispensable partner because of its human, agricultural, and industrial resources. Nor should it condemn Canada to such an unequal tête-à-tête with the powerful neighbour separated from it by only a slight border. Only Europe can prevent the economic absorption of Canada by the United States that would leave Ottawa but a weak political reflection of Washington. Outside Europe Canada is the only Western power able to maintain the delicate equilibrium that sways from one side of the Atlantic to the other. If Canada's weight falls on the American side of the scale, the balance will be forever lost. If it falls on the European side, then a chance – perhaps the last chance – of maintaining this balance will remain.

Neither Canada nor Europe wishes to break its ties with the United States. But Canada and Europe are trying to prevent their

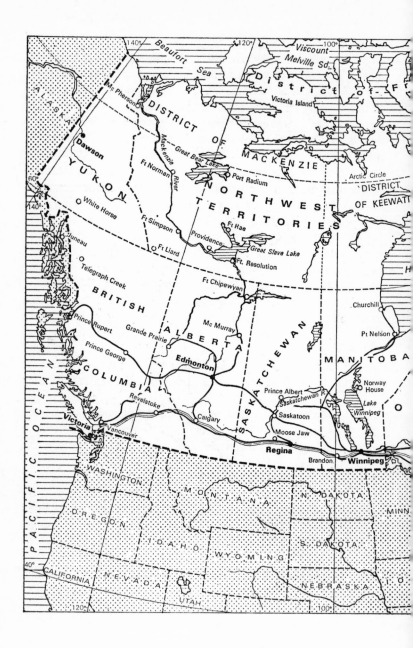

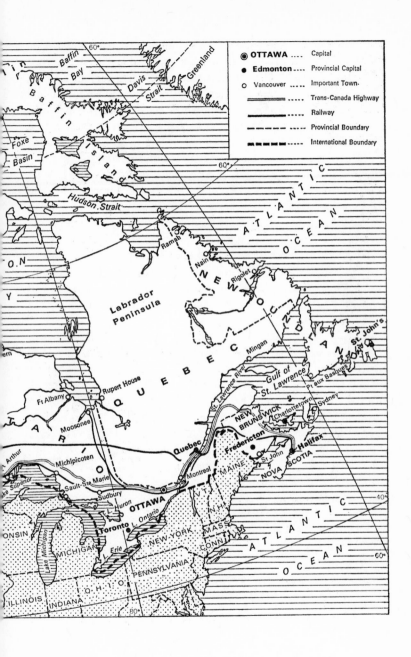

Legend:

◉ **OTTAWA** .... Capital
● **Edmonton** .... Provincial Capital
○ Vancouver ..... Important Town.
━━━━ ..... Trans-Canada Highway
━━━━ ..... Railway
─ ─ ─ ─ ..... Provincial Boundary
▬ ▬ ▬ ▬ ..... International Boundary

free alliance with the United States from degenerating to the level of vassal and sovereign. Despite the geographic distance, strong common ties unite Canada and Europe. If they remain divided, mutually ignoring one another, they will become impotent and will make of the alliance a body whose only centre lies in Washington. United, they could give the alliance two centres, with a flexibility and a vitality unknown today.

Canadians cannot blame a European for looking at their internal problems from this perspective. The grave crisis in relations between English and French Canadians has intrinsic interest for a sociologist. It touches a sensitive nerve in the Frenchman, who cannot help caring about the fate of these six million people across the Atlantic who speak his language and draw on the same cultural sources. Their existence and their vitality are a precious fund of light and enrichment for this language and culture. A Frenchman cannot help wondering whether Quebec will choose independence or whether it will play an active role within a renewed Confederation.

But the key question for the European is something else: will Canada allow itself to be colonized by the United States or will it strengthen its ties with Europe and help to balance the power of the United States? And, even if this is painful to the French Canadian, it must be said that assimilation of French Canada by English Canada would not change the wording of the question. For French Canada should be defending itself, not against twelve million English Canadians, but against the more than 200 million North Americans who speak English. By the same token, English Canadians should be upholding Canadian unity not against their compatriots in Quebec, but with French Canada against the enormous power of the United States.

Of course, a Frenchman has no reason to hope for the assimilation of Quebec. Instead, he rejoices to see it livelier, stronger, and more dynamic. But a Frenchman's – or a European's – interest in the eventual independence of Quebec is purely academic. Whether Quebec secedes or wins new status in Confederation, whether Canada flies apart in civil war or rebuilds its unity, France and Europe have only one thing at stake. Will Canada's resources be added to those of the United States to increase

American influence over Europe, or will Canada become the strength that Europe needs to set up a true dialogue with the United States?

The passionate way French Canadians argue their problems will interest nobody else until they look at them in this perspective. Separatists, who want an independent state of Quebec, use two arguments in their efforts to give their campaign an international context. First, they claim to be part of the great wave of colonial emancipation, and compare their struggles with those of Africans and Asians for national independence. But Quebec is not Ottawa's colony, nor is it Washington's; moreover, political independence would in no way guarantee economic independence from the United States. Second, they proclaim their desire to integrate an independent Quebec with an international French-language community, which they have even christened with the rather curious name of '*Commonwealth francophone*'. But they forget that, even though France obviously wants healthy and fruitful relationships with all French-speaking peoples, such ties in themselves cannot sustain France as a great power. That is why France looks beyond the constricted circle of French-speaking peoples to Europeans who speak German, Dutch, Italian; and that is why France and Europe need Canada, all of Canada – and all Canadians, whether they speak French or English.

And so, in trying to identify themselves with international movements, Quebec separatists merely prove they do not really understand them and do not yet know how to analyse realistically the relationships of power. They only underline the narrow provincialism of their preoccupations.

And yet the problems are real, their revolt is justified; on all evidence, French Canadians will not resign themselves to the future that has been allotted to them. The deep misunderstandings between English Canadians and French Canadians are virulent enough to menace the existence of Canada. Will this crisis give birth to a new and vigorous Canada, able to utilize its ties with Great Britain and France and avoid American hegemony? Or will it shatter the country, leaving the United States to pick up the pieces? More than Canada's future is at stake. The outcome of the crisis will either give Europe a vital ally or deny the old continent any hope of avoiding American domination. That is why this book, born of a certain irritation, is also pleading a cause.

Paris, July 1965

Unity and Independence

'Canada, without being fully conscious of the fact, is passing through the greatest crisis of its history.' Ten prominent Canadians, charged by their government with an important task, spent months travelling the country and gathering the facts and the opinions of thousands of citizens, only to conclude that the very existence of the country is seriously threatened. Already well aware of the problems, the members of the Royal Commission 'fully expected to find themselves confronted by tensions and conflicts. They knew that these difficulties have been current throughout the history of Confederation and can be expected in a country where cultures exist side by side.' But their inquiries revealed that the *malaise* was even stronger and more widespread than they had guessed.

What is this all about? On July 19, 1963, despite strong opposition from the Progressive Conservative Party, the Liberal government of Lester B. Pearson set up a royal commission, headed by André Laurendeau and Davidson Dunton, to undertake a mammoth study 'of the existing state of bilingualism and biculturalism in Canada'. He requested it to 'recommend what steps should be taken to develop the Canadian Confederation on the basis of an equal partnership between the two founding races, taking into account the contribution made by the other ethnic groups to the cultural enrichment of Canada.'

Eighteen months later, on February 1, 1965, the Laurendeau-Dunton Commission had not yet finished its work, but was so disturbed by its findings that it issued a preliminary warning. The preamble states: 'It would appear from what is happening now that the state of affairs established in 1867, which has never been seriously challenged, is now for the first time being rejected by the French Canadians of Quebec.' In 1867 the British North America Act created a federal state divided into four provinces (Ontario, Quebec, New Brunswick, and Nova Scotia), later joined by Manitoba (1870), British Columbia (1871), Prince Edward Island (1873), Saskatchewan and Alberta (1905), and Newfoundland (1949). And now, according to the Commission, this confederation is being called into question by the people of Quebec at the very moment when Canadians are preparing to celebrate their centennial.

Yet all seems calm in Quebec. Various groups, of course, have opened campaigns for secession. But their activities are carefully within the letter of the law, and their appeal does not seem to go beyond student and intellectual circles. The 'terrorists', who intended to use violence in the cause of separatism, have all been arrested, tried, and sentenced, and law and order are once again unbroken.

The Commission claims that this peacefulness is deceptive. It warns that if the crisis 'should persist and gather momentum, it could destroy Canada'. With its mandate from Parliament the Commission studied the respect actually being given to the principle of 'equal partnership between the two founding races', French and English. French Canadians claim that they are treated as a minority and not as an equal partner. And most English Canadians challenge the very principle of equality; they are twice as numerous as the French Canadians, and find it normal that the rule of the majority should result in English predominance. With this point of view they find Quebec's demands exorbitant. Can two peoples who so seriously disagree about such a grave matter still live together in the heart of one country, within the structure of one state?

The Commission is disturbed, yet not so pessimistic as to announce the forthcoming death of Canada. On the contrary, it sees this crisis as a chance to lance the abscess, to attack a problem that, until now, good taste has demanded be ignored. For, if this crisis 'is overcome, it will have contributed to the rebirth of a richer and more dynamic Canada. But this will be possible only if we face the reality of the crisis and grapple with it in time.'

To face the reality is the Commission's first task. And the

reality is that, although the 'two founding races' of Canada have lived together for two hundred years, they have not shared the same history. Surveying its history since Jacques Cartier landed at Gaspé (1534) and Champlain founded Quebec City (1603), since Nicolet explored the Great Lakes before Marquette and Jolliet and La Salle went down the Mississippi, since La Vérendrye discovered Lake Winnipeg in 1733 and ten years later reached the Rockies, 'Quebec tends to feel,' notes the Commission, 'that the French were settlers and the English invaders.' Today's drama has roots deep in the past. It explains why Quebec separatists in 1963 toppled the monument to Wolfe's victory over Montcalm two centuries ago on the Plains of Abraham. It explains why English and French Canadians attach so little importance to their common victories which in 1775-6 enabled them to turn back the Americans, but cannot forget the revolt of Papineau (1837). To the English, Lord Durham, who in 1839 recommended self-government, was the great decolonizer. To the French, he was the great assimilator who united Ontario and Quebec under one government. Louis Riel, the hero of the Métis insurrection in Manitoba, was for the French the victim of a 'judicial murder' that, to the English, was simply the execution of a common killer. And, in our own times, the conscription crises of 1917 and 1942 brought back to life ancient conflicts between English Canadians, who felt everyone should join in the common struggle for victory, and French Canadians, who balked at serving under the banner of His Britannic Majesty.

A history that should have united two peoples has instead divided them, and yet it has not quite managed to destroy their common destiny. Whether from England or France, Canadians know and intensely feel themselves to be a part of this North American continent, very different from the Europe whose ties they have not yet cast off. Shaped by the 'American way of life', and refusing to give citizens of the United States a monopoly on being American, they trace their ancestors to the pioneers who came from Portsmouth or Dieppe, treasuring either the traditions of the Mother of Parliaments or the pride of a spirit, language, and culture that distinguishes them from the two hundred million English-speaking North Americans.

DISSIMILAR NEIGHBOURS. Despite their quarrels and occasional bloody conflicts, the 'two founding races' are still strangely
similar in their fundamental preoccupations and objectives. The
immigrants who make up the population of the United States fled
the Europe of religious intolerance, despotism, persecution, and
famine, to build in freedom a new society in an immense land of
endless wealth. Millions of Irish, Jews, Poles, Italians, and re-
fugees from the Austro-Hungarian Empire rejected the misery
they had known in Europe and joined together in a common
faith in the individual. In direct contrast, the French who settled
in the St. Lawrence Valley were very conscious of believing in,
and bringing across the ocean, the values of the old country. After
the Concord incident the American revolutionaries, who in April
1775 hid behind the hedges to fire on the redcoats, announced the
independence of the colonies that refused to pay taxes imposed by
London and royal authority. But the fifty-thousand-odd Loyalists
who fled to Canada, where they formed the backbone of the small
English settlement, chose to obey rather than to flout the Crown.
French or English, Canadians cultivated the very ties with Europe
that the Americans wished to break. 'This is the deepest and most
meaningful difference between Canada and the United States,'
writes John Conway.[1] French and English Canadians, despite all
their differences, share an attachment to the monarchical form
of government and to a hierarchical form of Church structure –
be it Anglican or Roman Catholic. In the relationship between
authority and liberty, they emphasize authority. 'If these similarities between French and English had not effectively existed
beneath the endless surface ethnic and religious bickering, confederation would not only have been impossible, but incon-
ceivable,' Conway goes on to say.

And so, two apparently similar nations were growing up between the Rio Grande and the Arctic Circle, separated only by
an artificial border that seems to be easily crossed; two nations,
however, whose fundamental choices were contradictory. To
emigrate to Canada rather than to the United States involved a

---

[1]'What Is Canada?' in the *Atlantic Monthly,* November 1964, p. 100ff.
A Canadian by birth, John Conway taught for sixteen years at Harvard
before returning to York University in Toronto.

deliberate choice; the new arrivals came to the New World either in a spirit of faithfulness to Europe, or with the desire to break away. Usually, the choice was clear from the start. Sometimes it had to be made later. Nothing prevented the newcomer to Canada from crossing the 49th parallel; by the millions they have taken advantage of this possibility and settled in the United States, where they make up seventeen per cent of the immigrants admitted between 1850 and 1950. Knowing the fate of the minorities of New England and Louisiana, French Canadians who crossed the border to flee British domination were aware that the American republic offered them liberty with one string attached – progressive assimilation to the English language. As for English-speaking immigrants who settled in Canada rather than in the United States, they had physically left Great Britain, but spiritually and emotionally they still considered it their homeland. In their baggage they brought over fidelity to the Crown, the Union Jack, and the imposing solemnity of Victorian architecture. Americans nourished a vision of a new world while French and English Canadians met in a common desire to preserve their traditions. These traditions, of course, were influenced by the pioneer spirit, the open spaces, and the overflowing vitality of their neighbours to the south. But they remained strangely faithful to their roots while becoming authentically North American.

Two types of democracy grew up side by side. One asserted itself by revolution; the other took the slow path to independence in the best tradition of British pragmatism, waiting calmly until the second half of the twentieth century for the right to decide constitutional matters without reference to London. One was the daughter of eighteenth-century ideology, the other of nineteenth-century empiricism. 'We are getting rid of old world things and becoming accustomed to the new. We are forming new creeds, new judgments, new manners; we are becoming a new race of men,' wrote Charles Eliot Norton at the close of the Civil War. Canadians waited until 1964 to lay aside, and even then with a certain nostalgia, the Union Jack in favour of a new national flag – and the Quebec flag retains three royal fleurs-de-lis above the motto 'Je me souviens'. Inventors of a faith and a new society that they do not like to see challenged, the Americans are by vocation led to an absolute confidence in themselves which nourishes both their militant optimism and their Manichean view of the world. Formed by tradition and an evolutionary outlook, Canadians tend to admit the relative values of things and to temper all their analyses with a certain scepticism. Unlike their neighbours, they are never tempted to think themselves charged with a mission. Because of this, they offer less fertile ground for isolationism or witch-hunting. Granted, Canada as a middle power does not have the international responsibilities of the United States, yet the differences of policy between Ottawa and Washington flow mainly from the historic circumstances that have moulded the two national temperaments. Ties with Europe, most visible in Canada's membership in the Commonwealth, immunized Canada from extreme isolationism between the two world wars. Lacking the messianic spirit, Canadians, unlike Americans, have never considered Moscow, Peking, or Havana as capitals of Evil; they soften hard edges, they work for recognition of Red China, and, despite Washington's disapproval, they go on trading with Cuba. It is this more sober vision of the world, not the narrow border so easily pierced by press, radio, and television, that kept Canadians from the McCarthy hysteria of the United States. But the soul of a nation is not that simple, of course, and its complexity in Canada is translated into two main political parties. The Progressive Conservative Party, emphasizing ties with the Crown, stands for Canadian independence in the face of American expansion, though it is drawn closer to the United States by its anti-communist views. The Liberal Party, aware of its place in North America, has weaned Canada from British imperialism while at the same time resisting as much as it can pressures from Washington.

By their desire to remain faithful to Europe, the two founding races of Canada committed themselves to working out structures that would permit English and French to live together, all the while respecting each other's personality, language, and culture. On the other hand, their break with Europe impelled the Irish, Scots, Poles, Scandinavians, Germans, Italians, Russians, etc., who emigrated to the United States, to melt together into a new race, the American people. The melting-pot was not all-powerful;

it left by the wayside some dross that society could not assimilate, yet it grew by the desire of immigrants of all origins to adopt a common language and a set of customs and myths that gave birth to the American. The Canadian nation is founded on the coexistence of two peoples, and immigrants who arrive from countries other than England and France must integrate as best they can. The American nation makes one brew in which peoples of every land lose their original identity and acquire a new personality. Canada would be nothing but an American suburb if the wishes of the English Canadians who wanted to assimilate French Canada had prevailed. The harmonious co-operation of two founding peoples, both contributing to a common national heritage, is essential for Canada's survival on the doorstep of the United States. Attachment to two mother countries determined that the provinces, especially Quebec, would have wider powers than the member states of the Union. And while the crises and upsets of history in the United States have tended to reinforce federal authority, in Canada they have led, little by little, to greater provincial autonomy. In the name of 'states' rights', conservative forces in the United States have tried with little success to limit Washington's intervention in political, economic, social, and racial matters. In Canada, in the name of provincial autonomy, progressive forces have won from Ottawa important concessions, indispensable for the growth of the two linguistic and cultural groups. Emigrants who came to the United States from Europe to break with their past had to melt themselves into a homogeneous whole, which has progressively called for greater centralization of powers. Emigrants could only remain faithful to Europe in Canada, a country with decentralized structures that respected their individual characteristics.

The skyscrapers of Montreal and Toronto, small private homes, urban planning, the highway network, a certain type of publicity, the format of newspapers, etc., are an illusion; a thousand details of Canadian life are at first glance the 'American way of life', but Canada and the United States each has its own spirit, distinctive traditions, federal structure, and international outlook. The fact that Canada is a North American country does not make it merely a scale model of the United States.

Economics, along with history and political structures, adds to the distinctive characteristics of each country. Geographically larger than the United States but with only one-tenth the population, Canada is a major exporter of raw materials and importer of finished products. The United States imports raw materials from the entire world and exports only a small portion of its industrial production. Despite a high standard of living, Canada seems an underdeveloped country if you compare its industrial equipment with its still unexploited natural resources. In contrast, certain sectors of the American economy are overdeveloped, such as the steel industry, which normally operates at sixty per cent of capacity, and the United States, with its high level of consumption and the exhaustion of some natural resources, is obliged to import many raw materials: ferrous and non-ferrous metals, coal, textiles, wood, foodstuffs, etc.

AMERICAN ECONOMIC PREDOMINANCE. The economic differences btween the two neighbours tend to increase, rather than decrease, the ties that join them. Canada finds in the United States a major outlet for its raw materials, with a steadily growing demand and a close and accessible market. The United States is the obvious country to supply it with industrial equipment, machinery, and finished products. Trade between Canada and the United States grows in proportion to the growth of Canada's total foreign trade (see graph, p. 18).

Over the years, about 55 per cent of Canadian exports have gone to the United States, and about 67 per cent of its imports have come from the United States. This commercial predominance gives the United States enormous influence over the Canadian economy. Very few countries in the world have such an undiversified trade pattern. The situation affects Canada deeply; every recession, every hesitation in American economic activity, has its immediate counterpart in Canada.

The evolution of international trading has recently thwarted Canadian desire to be loyal to Europe. While the American share of Canadian trade remains constant, that of Great Britain and the Commonwealth is showing a clear tendency to fall, despite the system of Commonwealth preferences (see graph, p. 19). The table of Canada's main suppliers and customers from 1960 to 1964 (see pages 20 and 21) demonstrates, in absolute figures, a decline of $14.8 million in Canadian purchases from Great Britain, and an increase in Canadian sales to Great Britain of $284.6 million – representing a total increase in Anglo-Canadian trade

THE PREDOMINANT ROLE OF THE UNITED STATES IN CANADA'S FOREIGN TRADE

In 1964 52.7 per cent of Canada's exports went to the United States, which provided 68 per cent of Canada's imports. Despite slight fluctuations, shown in the table below, the United States consistently buys more than 50 per cent of Canada's exports and supplies up to 65 per cent of its imports.

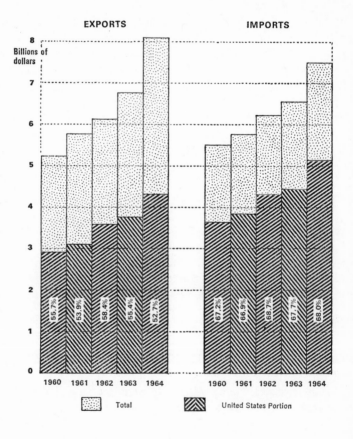

CANADIAN FOREIGN TRADE

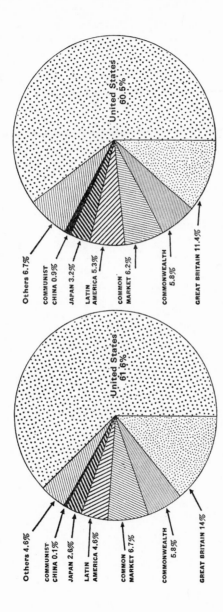

1960
($10,738 million)

1964
($15,587 million)

Others 4.6%
COMMUNIST CHINA 0.1%
JAPAN 2.6%
LATIN AMERICA 4.6%
COMMON MARKET 6.7%
COMMONWEALTH 5.8%
GREAT BRITAIN 14%
United States 61.6%

Others 6.7%
COMMUNIST CHINA 0.9%
JAPAN 3.2%
LATIN AMERICA 5.3%
COMMON MARKET 6.2%
COMMONWEALTH 5.8%
GREAT BRITAIN 11.4%
United States 60.5%

While the United States remains the principal partner in Canadian commerce, trade with Great Britain and the Commonwealth has actually lessened: these traditional ties are giving way to increased trade with Latin America, Japan, etc., though the massive wheat sales to Communist China represents only a tiny percentage of Canada's foreign trade. Trade with Eastern Europe has risen from 1.7 per cent in 1963 to 3.2 per cent in 1964.

of $269.8 million. This figure is insignificant when compared with the total increase in Canadian trade for the same period – more than $4,800 million. If this trend continues, it will mean that Canada's membership in the Commonwealth, which has so far given Canada a distinctive character, will have less and less practical effect. Historical, sentimental, and cultural ties would probably break down along with the economic ones, leaving Canada without any major defence against the dynamic American economy.

Despite a slight increase in volume of trade with the Common Market countries, their percentage of Canada's total trade has fallen from 6.7 per cent in 1960 to 6.2 per cent in 1964. New markets in Latin America, Japan, and Communist China (wheat

The United States – Canada's Major Supplier
(in millions of dollars)

	1960	1961	1962	1963	1964
United States	3,686.6	3,863.9	4,299.5	4,444.9	5,164.4
Great Britain	588.9	618.2	563	526	574.1
Venezuela	195.1	216.6	224.2	243.4	270.6
Japan	110.3	116.6	125.3	130.4	174.4
West Germany	126.9	136.5	141.1	144	170.4
France	50.1	54.2	56.1	58.1	69.0
Italy	42.8	49.1	51.8	55.3	67.5
Australia	35.5	36.6	45.2	55.6	60.0
Belgium, Luxembourg	41.4	44.7	48.6	47.3	59.2
Jamaica	37.6	38.5	39.7	51.5	47.8
India	29.3	33.4	43.4	53	36.1
Saudi Arabia	37.4	41.3	40.5	50.2	18.5
Iran	30.7	21.6	31.7	42.7	31.1
TOTAL	5,482.7	5,768.6	6,257.8	6,558.8	7,489.6

The table reveals an increase in eastern Canada's purchase of Venezuelan oil (western Canada is rich in oil) and bauxite from Jamaica for the aluminum plants at Arvida, Quebec, and at Kitimat, British Columbia. Since 1960 the value of purchases from the United States has risen in absolute figures and in percentage of the total, while that of the second largest supplier, Great Britain, has fallen by $14.8 million.

sales) are not enough to revitalize the shape of Canada's foreign trade. The United States is far and away Canada's major supplier and customer, despite Ottawa's efforts at diversification. If Canada is to maintain a measure of independence in the face of the American mammoth, Great Britain, along with the Commonwealth and the Common Market, must have a larger share of Canada's foreign trade. This explains the interest in a billion-dollar project that would allow France to buy 50,000 tons of Canadian uranium over twenty years. Such contracts would give Canada an opening into other markets and would help it to establish a better economic balance. Thus it is no surprise that the United States has raised objections to the project, invoking the need to control the uses of uranium.

The United States – Canada's Major Customer
(in millions of dollars)

	1960	*1961*	*1962*	*1963*	*1964*
United States	2,932.1	3,107.1	3,608.4	3,766.3	4,271.1
Great Britain	915.2	909.3	909	1,006.8	1,199.8
Japan	178.8	231.5	214.5	296	330.2
U.S.S.R.			3.2	150.1	315.9
West Germany	165.5	188.6	177.6	170.9	211.5
Australia	98.8	78.6	104.9	100.7	145.8
Communist China	8.7	125.4	147.4	104.7	136.3
Netherlands	62.5	61.2	76.9	87	101.6
Belgium, Luxembourg	69.1	76	68.1	76.4	100.5
France	72.9	71.9	57.5	63.3	79.4
Italy	68.3	67.6	74.5	76.7	
Norway	61.5	69.7	69	73	
TOTAL	5,255.6	5,755	6,178.5	6,798.5	8,094.8

From 1960 to 1964 the American share in Canadian exports has increased by $1,339 million, which is nevertheless a decrease from 55.7 per cent to 52.7 per cent of the total. Great Britain's share, despite an increase of $284 million, declined from 17.4 per cent to 14.9 per cent of the total.

The United States, a great consumer of raw materials, is also a great source of capital, which it likes to invest in the least troubled areas of the world. Canada, tailor-made for such investment, has attracted an estimated $20 billion – double the sum of American investment in all Latin America. This inflow of capital is the main reason for the increase in Canada's foreign debt – from $5 billion in 1951 to $27.8 billion in 1961. And as a result, an important part of Canadian industry is directly controlled by American capital. 'I do not believe,' said Walter Gordon, Minister of Finance, 'that this is a healthy situation.'[1] His euphemism should leave no doubt as to the uneasiness of the Canadian government. Moreover, Mr. Gordon made his opinion very clear when he added:

> In the early 1950s, when great expansion characterized all sectors of the Canadian economy, one could begin to count key industries where relatively few companies, under foreign control, in some way dominated the industry. Outside firms, for example, dominated the petroleum and natural gas industry. They had taken over the development of aluminum, iron ore and asbestos, most sectors of the chemical industry, and at least three important secondary industries – automobile, electrical appliances and rubber products. Since the early 1950s, direct foreign investments have continued to flow into Canada in important quantities. In certain key sectors of our economy, foreign ownership and control has reached high proportions. According to the most recent statistics, those of 1961, foreign investors control about 70 per cent of the sales of petroleum and natural gas, about 59 per cent of mines and foundries, and about 60 per cent of manufacturing. That means that not only are the important decisions about Canadian industry made by people who live outside our borders, but that our industrial companies are directly affected by events that take place elsewhere. For example, the most important company in Ontario recently had to shut down because its parent company in the United States was strike-bound.

This last example was hardly needed to make Mr. Gordon's meaning clear to his audience. European investment in Canada is so modest that everyone knows 'foreign investment' really means 'American investment'. To give only two examples, foreigners control 75 per cent of the Canadian petroleum and natural gas industry and 61 per cent of the mining industry – and

[1] Speech by Walter Gordon in Peterborough, Ontario, on October 28, 1964.

the American share in these two sectors is respectively 70 per cent and 52 per cent. The major sectors of Canadian industry (see chart on this page) are thus controlled by foreign capital, and the great share of that capital is American.

The United States has made possible rapid development of the Canadian economy by supplying not only the necessary funds, but also the technical, scientific, and administrative expertise

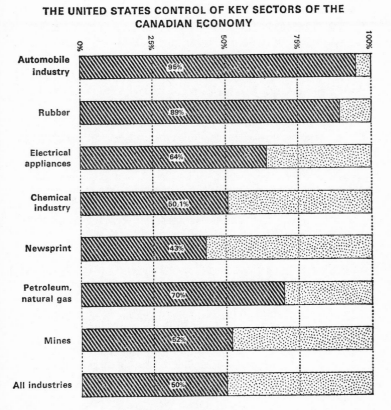

THE UNITED STATES CONTROL OF KEY SECTORS OF THE CANADIAN ECONOMY

'Important decisions about Canadian industry are made by people living outside our borders,' declared Walter Gordon, Canadian Minister of Finance, on October 28, 1964. He added: 'Canada will not be able to maintain its independence without paying the price.'

that was lacking. However, as Mr. Gordon points out, 'let us not pretend that this help has been an unmixed blessing.' For, 'in no other developed country in the world can you find such a high proportion of the industry controlled from outside.'

The Second World War and the Korean War strongly encouraged the United States, looking for raw materials, to invest in Canada. But the tendency is older than that. From 1900 to 1913, American foreign investment rose from $500 to $2,500 million, of which 50 per cent went to Latin America and 25 per cent to Canada.[1] It was the zenith of dollar diplomacy – an approach repudiated by President Wilson in 1913, but still a lively and effective reality. The economic crisis of 1929-30 put the brakes on the export of capital, but the needs of military production during the Second World War and the Korean War gave new impetus to foreign investment. Canada attracted American funds with its natural resources of uranium, petroleum, and non-ferrous metals. Large American companies set up branch offices in Canada, another mixed blessing, for, after the Korean armistice, the aviation companies that had been producing Sabre jet fighters had to lay off most of their personnel.

American investment in Canada seldom takes the form of bonds or other fixed-interest securities redeemable at maturity. Americans usually buy shares that cannot be bought back unless their foreign holder wishes to sell. 'The inflow of capital has contributed to the growth of the country and borrowing for this purpose is justified,' said Walter Gordon. 'But it becomes a subject for debate when investment involves yielding shares to foreigners who thereby obtain the right to make decisions affecting our lives and our interests.'

By selling raw materials and buying finished products, Canada ends up with a yearly deficit in its balance of trade with the United States. The Minister of Finance saw the danger of this situation: 'From 1958 to 1962,' said Mr. Gordon, 'we had unused natural resources and a large number of unemployed. Yet we continued to acquire foreign debts and to sell our Canadian companies for the money to pay for our imports. It makes no

[1] J. B. Duroselle, *De Wilson à Roosevelt, politique extérieure des Etats-Unis,* Armand Colin, 1960.

sense. In effect, we were importing unemployment.' The only way to remedy the situation would be to finance industrialization with savings and repay foreign debts, undergoing, if need be, a period of austerity that would be politically awkward but economically inevitable.

Until that happens, Canadian prosperity fluctuates with the American economy and decisions made in the United States. Thus, in 1960-2 Canada's uranium sales fell from $263 to $166 million, and several mines had to close. In addition, in order to limit unemployment in the United States, every recession of the American economy is first countered by a slowdown in the activity of Canadian branch offices. In the same way, Washington's decision to forbid sales of so-called strategic materials to communist countries was applied to the Canadian branches of American companies, thus affecting the entire Canadian economy.

'A Canadian subsidiary of an American flour milling company cannot sell Canadian-made flour to China without putting the president of the American parent company in danger of being sent to jail,' wrote Robert M. Fowler. 'A Canadian company is unable to trade in full compliance with Canadian laws because of the extraterritorial effect of an American statute. It is very irritating to Canadians to have American-controlled companies in Canada used in this way to implement American foreign policy.'[1] This rule even applies, of course, to countries like Cuba, with which Canada has maintained normal diplomatic relations. Thus, industries installed in Canada, using Canadian skill to process Canadian raw materials, cannot sell their products according to Canada's economic and political interests. No wonder there are Canadians who say their country is a colony of the United States. They would not mind if a small part of their economy was controlled by American capital, but they are alarmed at the size of American control over their means of production.

The government in Ottawa has taken various measures to decrease this heavy dependence. So far, these measures have been timid and ineffectual. The presence of Canadian citizens in the

[1]'The Impact of American Business', by Robert M. Fowler, in the *Atlantic Monthly*, November 1964.

administration of these companies does not prevent the really important decisions' being made in the United States. Moreover, the recommendation that the large branch offices in Canada sell 20 to 25 per cent of their capital shares to Canadians remains a pious wish. Even were it to be carried out, it would not solve the basic problem. Canada's Minister of Finance was quite correct when he pointed out that other countries, notably in Europe, have taken more radical steps to assure themselves a certain freedom of movement. 'However,' he added, 'none of those countries was in quite our situation, where the burden of foreign ownership is much more marked since it is concentrated in one single powerful country – even if we do have warm, neighbourly relations with that country.'

These warm, neighbourly relations, however, do not prevent more or less direct political pressure. For one thing, the enormous American food surpluses which, under the Food for Peace Plan, can be sold at absurdly low prices constitute a permanent threat to foreign sales of Canadian foodstuffs. Most of all, the commercial aspect is always carefully weighed when the Ottawa government considers any move that might displease Washington. Although other motives such as Western solidarity are the official reason, fear of economic reprisals (which would not be presented as such) explains why Canada has not carried out certain of its desires – such as diplomatic recognition of Peking.

This is why Walter Gordon could state, in careful diplomatic phrases:

> Canada will not be able to maintain its independence without paying the price. . . . No country in the world can boast of its independence if it is not master of its own communications media, its financial institutions, and, one way or another, of the general decisions made by the directors of its important industries. . . . No country, including Canada, can hope for political independence if it allows the citizens of others countries too large a part of its economic power.

THE TWO PILLARS. Canada's economic and political independence conditions its loyalty to its purpose and historic traditions. Simple geography ties Canada and the United States closely together in a common strategy for the defence of North America.

The two countries have established a unified command and radar networks right to the Arctic. History, according to a currently popular theory, would have liked to make Canada the bridge between England and the United States; but, in war or peace, the two countries are quite obviously close allies who need no intermediary. In fact, for the past twenty years Canada's international role has had quite a different emphasis. It is a middle power, respected by the big and trusted by the small and accepted by both parties to a dispute, be it Vietnam or Suez, in the U.N. or in NATO. Canadian diplomacy uses this basis of strength with intelligence and ingenuity, and has often opened the way to compromise and conciliation toward greater world peace. Such a role has its limits, the limits of Canada's real independence. A man who has long participated at the high-level formation of this diplomacy is particularly well qualified to judge it with cold realism: 'There is always the danger,' writes John W. Holmes, Director General of the Canadian Institute of International Affairs, 'that if Canada flouts United States' feelings too far, an ill-disposed Congress would take a harsh view on the many economic questions affecting Canada. Canada is vulnerable to the risk of economic reprisals even though the United States administration is too decent to threaten them.'[1] The bitter memory of uncomfortable experiences breaks through even the polished language of the diplomat; memories of interference by Washington's influence in Ottawa, imposed discreetly, perhaps, but none the less effective, are evident.

American capital already controls a large part of the major sectors of the Canadian economy. Should the situation worsen and Canada become a mere economic branch office of the United States, its national and international sovereignty would be reduced to a sham. Ottawa can maintain and increase its freedom by progressive reorientation of its foreign trade and by an active search for European and Japanese capital – anything, in short,

[1]'The Diplomacy of a Middle Power', by John W. Holmes, Director General of the Canadian Institute of International Affairs, former Acting Permanent Representative of Canada to the United Nations, former Under-Secretary of State for External Affairs. In the *Atlantic Monthly*, November 1964.

that would help break the present unequal Canadian-American relationship.

Or is it already too late? Europe has long ignored this far-off ally which it thinks of as a quaint, folkloric anachronism, never realizing the immense and largely unexploited resources hidden in the vast reaches of Canadian soil between the Atlantic and the Pacific, the Great Lakes and the Arctic. The English tend to treat Canada as a lovely ornament in their crown, a faithful partner that merits the occasional royal visit. They have written off its great natural resources as the property of the United States, when these resources ought to be offered first to the Commonwealth. The French, hypnotized by Africa and their need to maintain their footing in the Common Market, are even more isolationist and naive; Canada is for them a blustery climate where some 'cousins' show a touching determination to go on speaking French. They do not know that from 1939 to 1963 Canada's Gross National Product multiplied eight-fold, jumping from $5.6 to $43 million. France once lost Canada to England. Now, if they are not careful, France and England will lose Canada to the United States. And this loss, for the whole of Europe, will be much more serious than the defeat of Montcalm was for France.

Although Canada is rich thanks to the resources already exploited, the greatest part of these resources is as yet untapped. It is the world's third-largest producer of wheat (after the U.S.S.R. and the United States), harvesting twice as much as France and half as much as the United States, though having a population one-tenth the size. But it is Canada's mineral resources that offer the greatest potential for development. It is already the world's largest producer of asbestos (45 per cent of the world's total), nickel (232,000 tons, which is three-quarters of the world's yearly demand and worth almost $400 million a year), platinum, and zinc (530,000 tons). It is second in the production of uranium, gold, cadmium, gypsum, and titanium, and third, immediately after Australia and the United States, in the production of lead, magnesium, cobalt, and bismuth. Thanks to hydro-electric resources, Canada is second only to the United States in the production of aluminum with 700,000 tons a year. It is a major producer of copper (460,000 tons), silver, iron ore (28 million tons exported, 80 per cent to the United States), and petroleum (800,000 barrels a day, one-third exported to the United States). In addition, immense forests make Canada one of the world's major sources of wood, paper, and newsprint.

Moreover, these stark figures give only a slight idea of its wealth. The possibilities are staggering. At the start of this century Canadian mineral production was worth $64 million; in 1963 it was worth $2,950 million. Canada is now forty-six times beyond its 1900 level. To choose another yardstick, the value of mineral production *per capita* has more than doubled from $76 to $157 between 1950 and 1963. No less significant is the increase in iron-ore production: 1.1 million tons in 1945, 16.3 million tons in 1955, and finally 28 million tons in 1963. Petroleum production has risen from 7 million barrels a day in 1946 to 290 million barrels in 1963.

However impressive it may be as an illustration of the rapid developments in the mining industry, this rising curve also predicts even more remarkable advances in the near future. The geological map of Canada is still far from complete, and each month, each week, it is marked with new discoveries whose dimensions are still uncharted. Thus the world's richest potassium deposit was recently discovered in Saskatchewan, where the Esterhazy mine, with an annual capacity of 1,200,000 tons, is the most important in North America. Even though the resources in southern Canada are not yet fully exploited, as methods of prospecting improve, the boundary of known deposits moves steadily northward. The Canadian Shield, whose treasures have not yet been accurately estimated, hides far more wealth than was suspected even by the gold and silver miners who scrambled to Rossland, Kimberley, and Porcupine.

Why has Europe been so incredibly indifferent to the economic treasure-chest of Canada? One factor is that Canada's most spectacular development has occurred since the Second World War; mineral production increased six-fold from 1945 to 1963. Moreover, as soon as peace returned, Europe had to give priority to its own reconstruction. Once this was accomplished, Europe tended to consider Canada the private hunting-ground of the

United States. The Americans have invested more than $20 billion in the Canadian economy. This figure alone is impressive, but Canada's underground riches call for even larger investment. The near-monopoly American capital already has on Canadian natural resources assures it a dominant position. But it would be wrong to consider the game already played and lost; the economic potential of Canada leaves the door open to a vast inflow of capital, technicians, and specialized workers. Will this new effort be carried out by the United States, assuring it a position of near-monopoly, or will Europe decide to enter the contest and secure for itself a suitable position?

Canadians are too well aware of their dependence on the United States not to wish for European investment. They know their economic potential will not remain unexploited and they would like more than one foreign country to be involved. Their appeals to Europe so far have found little response – perhaps because Europe looks on a request for aid as a beggar's call for charity. This could not be less accurate. For while the aid Europe could offer is undoubtedly Canada's only chance to escape American domination, it would also give Europe a hope of standing up to American power.

So many factors – the divisions of Europe, the tendency of certain countries to follow in the wake of the United States, the superior military strength of the United States – make it difficult for a true dialogue between equal partners to take place across the Atlantic. But the progress (though undoubtedly too slow) of European unification and the fact that the United States knows it has a military and a political need for Europe still allow Europe to make its voice heard.

This fragile equilibrium will be destroyed if Canada finally falls under American control. The United States would then have such overwhelming economic superiority that Europe would no longer be able to resist Washington or to defend its own ideas. The vitality of the Atlantic alliance presupposes confrontation and free discussion between its members. If American power is enriched by Canadian potential – if the economic frontier of the United States, while respecting the fiction of a political boundary, moves to the Canadian far north – then the delicate Atlantic equilibrium will be destroyed and the American giant will be unopposed in the West. Washington has already opposed the 'two pillar' theory of NATO with a monolithic concept of its own. But it would no longer even be a subject for discussion if American power were to be swollen with Canadian riches. Europe could talk on, but it would not be heard.

If Europe finally decides to make significant investments in Canada, not only will it be helping Canada defend its political independence from the United States, but it will be helping save its own. The very balance of the West is at stake. When Jean Monnet received the Freedom Prize in New York on January 23, 1963, he passionately urged 'an association of *equal partners* between Europe and the United States'. And he explained, 'Such an association is necessary for world peace and for continued freedom.' But it is not enough to proclaim the equality of partners; this equality must be based on solid economic and political realities. That demands not only the cohesion of Western Europe, but also all the support Europe can muster in Canada. It would be useless to protest that the United States sometimes uses its power to suppress its allies. It is far more to the point to work for a true balance of power within the alliance. Here Canada has a key role; other than the United States it is the only country in North America, and Europe's attitude will determine whether Canada's economic potential will strengthen American power or help to counterbalance it.

Certain American executives would have good cause to worry about any diminution of their power. But they are up against other Americans who agree with John F. Kennedy's opinion: 'We don't look upon a strong and united Europe as a rival, but as an associate. . . . We see in such a Europe an associate with whom we can carry out, *on a basis of full equality,* all the heavy and important tasks which touch on the health and defence of a community of free nations.'[1] Or, put another way, it is a question of 'full equality' between Europe and the United States. Either the alliance leans on the United States, or it develops on 'two pillars' of almost equal strength. The vitality of an alliance is

[1] J. F. Kennedy, Philadelphia speech, July 4, 1962.

in its flexibility, not in its monolithic structure, and flexibility depends on free discussion between equal partners. The choice between the two concepts depends on Europe. It would be crushed by a monolith; with the 'two pillars' idea it could keep alive the possibility of dialogue by reinforcing its own internal unity and helping Canada to protect its economic and political independence.

The future of the Old World and of Canada are intertwined, but few Canadians see the future of their country in these terms. Weighed down by their internal French-English problem, they have ignored their major problem, even though they are well aware of it – their economic and consequently political dependence on the United States. It is quite true, as the *Preliminary Report* of the Laurendeau-Dunton Commission states, that the very existence of the country is in doubt because of the mutual incomprehension of the 'two founding races'. But however grave it may be, the problem is not insoluble. Whether or not Canada remains one country, the real question is whether the riches of Canada will fall to the United States or not. A major part of the economy, thanks to European indifference, has passed under the control of American capital. The influence of Washington on Ottawa is all the stronger for it. A divided Canada would merely be easier prey for American interests. Quebec separatists would escape Ottawa's 'control' only to fall under Washington's. The possible balance between Europe and the United States would be lost.

The independence of Canada, which influences the form of the West, depends both on Europeans and on Canadians. It is high time Europe took an active, useful interest in Canada by developing commercial exchanges and by sending funds and technicians. It is high time Canadians saw their problems on the world scale. John Diefenbaker, leader of the Progressive Conservative Party, may well think the Laurendeau-Dunton Commission *Report* nothing but a 'mass of generalities and platitudes'. The *Report* has none the less brought to light the essential elements of the crisis. In the province of Quebec, stated the Commissioners, 'we did not hear from anyone . . . who was an avowed defender of the status quo.' The problems must be faced, not merely covered over once again. For, as the Commission rightly pointed out, if the crisis is overcome, it will have 'contributed to the rebirth of a wealthier and more dynamic Canada'. This dynamism and wealth are indispensable to the balance between the United States and Europe. Canadians ought to realize this; it would help them work out solutions to their internal problems. Quebec sets forth the problems, claiming that present structures are ill-equipped to handle today's needs. And if Quebec plays the driving role, this is because it has pulled itself out of vain regrets and set itself on the road to progress. At the heart of the Canadians crisis, but equally at the heart of new solutions for the future, is a revolution that nobody could have foreseen thirty years ago. Quebec is making itself a new skin; Quebec is emerging from the past.

Quebec Emerges from the Past

In 1963 a group of young activists put bombs in mailboxes in Westmount, a Montreal suburb, but their names will not go down in history. The miracle is that the echo of those bombs was heard right across the country, provoking English Canadians more to annoyance than to uneasiness. The world has known the Nazi concentration camps, the annihilation of Dresden, the senseless holocaust of Hiroshima, the horrors of the Algerian war, Congo massacres, and two dirty wars in Indo-China; in comparison, a few sticks of dynamite in Montreal are petty indeed. After the arrests of the Quebec activists no one came forward to bear out the words of their rallying-song:

> Here, each knows what he wants and what he must do,
> Friend, if you fall, a friend from the shadows replaces you.

Their organization in no way resembles the network of the French resistance under Nazi occupation, or current liberation movements or groups of partisans. For, whatever they say, they are simply not in the position of a country that is occupied by a foreign army or that is colonized. By proclaiming themselves 'terrorists' they usurped a vocabulary that does not belong to them and demonstrated their ignorance of their own situation and that of a world caught in the fever of revolution.

The drama of the young people in the Quebec Liberation Front (F.L.Q.) is their false identification with the Viet Cong or the Algerian F.L.N. They had chosen not to take other lives – a night watchman, killed by accident, was the only victim – and not to risk their own. This limited form of violence created a shadowy movement, much less spectacular and much less effective than the non-violent action of Negroes in the United States.

36

Despair alone cannot make heroes. This was clearly apparent when, in the same year, 1963, the hunger strike of a non-violent separatist, Marcel Chaput, took place amid public indifference and ended on an inglorious note.

In a country with the third-highest standard of living in the world (after the United States and Sweden), it is as hard to play Gandhi as it is to play Fidel Castro. The young F.L.Q. members played with words when they proclaimed that their 'terrorist' action would 'liberate' them from their 'colonial' position. Yet they had some distinguished backing for their misuse of language. Jacques Berque, a professor at the Collège de France, wrote after a visit to Quebec, 'Here we see the same insurrection which . . . .'[1] But there was no 'insurrection'. The 'terrorism' never got beyond the stage of noisy, rather than murderous, agitation – simply because Quebec cannot be considered a 'colonial' area.

Quebec separatists certainly did not wait for Jacques Berque to invoke, in the name of their cause, the example of former colonies being given independence. 'Never, in the history of the world,' wrote one of their organizers, Marcel Chaput,[2] 'has it been easier for conquered peoples to achieve independence. Since the end of the Second World War, as we have often repeated, more than thirty countries have won their independence. We live in the middle of the twentieth century, the golden age of independence. People scarcely out of the stone age have obtained the independence they desired. And we, French Canadians, sons of the great French civilization, sons of colonists and pioneers who . . . .'

But Quebec separatism is not simply the product of the wave of emancipation that has swept through colonized peoples following the Second World War. Even if the examples of Guinea and Ghana have encouraged it, its roots are deep in the situation of Quebec itself. It arose there because of conditions existing within the province and because of its place within the whole of Confederation.[3] These two aspects must be examined in order to

[1]*France-Observateur,* October 10, 1963.
[2]Marcel Chaput, *Pourquoi je suis séparatiste,* Editions du Jour, Montreal, 1961, pp. 109-10.
[3]See page 134 for the chart showing the relationship, by population and economy, of Quebec to the other provinces.

understand the origins, the nature, and the perspective of separatism.

TWENTY YEARS OF PATERNALISM. Dominating the St. Lawrence, which leads ships from the high seas to the Great Lakes in the heart of the continent, the old citadel seems unchanging. With its grey stones, fleurs-de-lis, red, black, and gold *calèches*, weathered bronze statues of royal captains and of *coureurs de bois*, and winding streets, Quebec, that little bit of Europe in the New World, ever looks the same. Huge North American buildings have hardly marred the harmony of the soft lines, warmly human and gently old-fashioned. The change lies within, deep within a people who, all of a sudden, are restless and awake, asserting themselves, and balking. And soon, events that would have been unthinkable a few years earlier began to take place; in Quebec secretaries in the outer office of a minister pretended not to understand a single word spoken by some visitors who knew only English. In the stores and restaurants, of course, everybody has a warm welcome for the English-speaking client. As in South America, everyone who lives by commerce and tourism knows how to flatter the Yankee. In Quebec, on the very Plains of Abraham where Montcalm was mortally wounded, the traffic signs are bilingual. But everywhere a new pride expresses a quickening of wounded dignity. The English language paves the French Canadian's way to high salaries in industry and finance, but given the chance, he is quick to recall that bilingualism should work both ways. And so the English Canadian discovers with amazement that his superiority is being challenged. Something has changed on the shores of the St. Lawrence.

French-Canadian nationalism is nothing new. It flares up periodically in a population fiercely jealous of its own identity. But it seems to have taken a new direction, with greater confidence and strength. As after an interminable winter, a people appears to be shaking off its torpor, blinking in the sunlight, and opening the way to a new adventure. This adventure began at the end of the summer of 1959 when Maurice Duplessis, who for twenty years was the absolute master of the Union Nationale Party and of Quebec, died. Duplessis maintained his power by flattering French-Canadian nationalism. But his acts contradicted his demagoguery. He exalted the 'French fact', all the while turning a suspicious eye on republican, secular France – an object of horror for a religious province whose emblem is the royalist fleur-de-lis. He cultivated a certain chauvinism among his people, yet he used provincial power over education to maintain an abysmal educational system which could not even teach the French language properly, let alone promote French culture. Suspicious of everyone else, he turned over the natural resources of his province to foreign capital, which in turn made large donations to his electoral war-chest. How could he fool his fellow-citizens for so long? Only a small minority, receptive to the outside world, dared a systematic denunciation of Duplessis, and their work began to show results only after his death.

Some people have tried to work out a shaky parallel between the premier and such Latin American dictators as Somoza or Batista. Corruption was raised to the level of a government technique, and fraudulent contracts fattened the Union Nationale bank accounts. Each election night henchmen watched over the ballot-boxes, which were about to yield the expected victory. But if some Quebeckers talked about 'tyranny', it was because they did not know the violence of the Caribbean. Duplessis's power was based quite simply on paternalism and clericalism, and most of his people accepted both.

The amazing personality of Maurice Duplessis had a profound influence on Quebec. Absolute master of the province, somewhat like Huey Long, who before him had been the 'dictator' in Louisiana, he reigned through corruption but without any desire for personal gain. Power was enough and he kept it with iron determination. In 1952 he wrenched his spinal column and governed the province for two months from a hospital bed. Still incapacitated at election-time, he donned a steel brace and stumped the province as usual. This was enough to make an American journalist write that 'nothing less than death, senility or overwhelming public rejection could force him to yield power'.[1] In the end it was death.

'If there's a good government,' he used to say, 'you don't need

[1] Craig Thompson, in *Look*, April 24, 1954.

an opposition.' And his would-be opponents knew very well that they were inviting pitiless revenge. To please certain Catholic groups Duplessis pushed through a law allowing the imprisonment of Jehovah's Witnesses. The Montreal *restaurateur* who put up bail for them soon found himself without the all-important liquor licence and had to close down his business.

Duplessis's hostility to trade unions and his use of public power against strikers won him important contributions from bankers and businessmen. Trafficking in liquor licences was another major source of revenue. But the biggest source was kickbacks on contracts for public works, through the device of inflated estimates. This money did not go to Duplessis personally but to the Union Nationale war-chest, to be used for various forms of bribery. The premier could thus give his birthplace, Trois Rivières, a beautiful bridge which he opened by declaring, 'This bridge is as straight and as strong as the Union Nationale.' It collapsed soon after, an inquiry commission attributing the accident to 'unknown causes'. In fact, after paying off his various patrons – including the Union Nationale – and making sure of his own profit, the contractor had little money left for preliminary studies and quality construction materials.

A demagogue, Duplessis dismissed as 'Bolsheviks' the members of a Catholic union that set off the 1949 asbestos strike[1] and those who supported it, including the Archbishop of Montreal, Mgr. Charbonneau, and the faculty of social sciences at Laval University. Mgr. Charbonneau took up a collection in his diocese for the strikers. He lost his archbishopric.

All his life, Duplessis fought to gain, then to keep, power – at any price. In 1927 at the age of thirty-seven he was elected for the first time, as a Conservative. His party had lost much of its popularity by supporting conscription during the 1914-18 war. However, by 1933 Duplessis had become 'chief' of the party; he subsequently destroyed it, created the Union Nationale, and controlled the new party machine absolutely. Three years later he won a majority in the provincial legislature after a cam-

[1]The city of Asbestos, 100 miles east of Montreal, is in the heart of a region that supplies 94 per cent of Canadian asbestos production and 38 per cent of total world production. It is the most important deposit in the world.

paign that had told all of Quebec, 'You want a bridge, a road, a school? You can get them with your ballots. Vote for the Union Nationale and you'll get what you want.' His arguments were seldom more subtle, seldom less convincing.

Premier from 1936 to 1939, he did not want to make the same mistake the Conservatives had made during the First War, and, in calling the expected provincial election, he promised to keep Quebec out of any world conflict. The Liberal response was just as vigorous; Duplessis must be driven from power or else the Liberal members from Quebec in the federal parliament would resign, leaving French Canadians without any parliamentary voice in the conscription issue.

Duplessis lost that election but returned to power in 1944, before the end of the war. He was to be in power for fifteen years more. His methods did not change. In 1948, to win re-election, he invented a supposed Ottawa plot to Anglicize all Canada. This red herring won him 82 out of 92 seats in the Quebec legislature. The victory was beyond his wildest hopes. Now he knew that nationalism was his never-failing weapon. Without scruple he flattered Quebec patriotism with his voice and accelerated its economic 'colonization' with his deeds.

This whole attitude is beautifully illustrated by the agreement Duplessis reached with the American Iron Ore Company for rights to the rich iron deposits discovered in the Ungava region. The deal involved five million acres of land and more than 400 million tons of iron ore (content 55 per cent). Production is about 15 million tons a year. But the Iron Ore Company's payments to Quebec are in no way related to production; they are fixed at $100,000 a year, or one dollar per 150 tons. The price is obviously ridiculous, even if the Company did have to put out some $250 million for a port, a railway line from Schefferville to Sept-Iles, etc. Such concessions obviously are more closely related to pillage than to development, and obviously no government would consider renewing the agreement under the terms accepted by Duplessis. As a result Quebec has decided to create its own steel industry.

Since the end of 1959 and the death of Duplessis a sort of continuing explosion has been shaking the old structures which

had seemed settled for all time. Pent-up energies were suddenly set loose. The halter had been velvet-lined, but rigid. The
premier's death blew it apart. And in every field, those who had
felt themselves checked, harassed, suffocated under a heavy
paternalism, suddenly rediscovered the intoxication of freedom.
In every way – political, intellectual, religious – the whole province exploded. In the face of all this, the highest civil and
religious authorities, either out of conviction or out of oppor-
tunism, gave way. If authoritarianism has not yielded all its rights,
at least it no longer holds the upper hand.

French Canadians owe to the Church the preservation of their
language and their faith in a Protestant and Anglo-Saxon environment. Yet a lay movement has sprung up whose leaders
express themselves freely on radio and television. They nibble
away at the traditional field of the Church; they publish mani-
festos, hold conferences, find Catholics who will debate with
them, and demand and are close to obtaining lay schools. The
reaction against clerical abuses finds supporters among believers
as well as atheists, and even in the ranks of the clergy. The wave
is so strong that many young people are rejecting the faith along
with the clericalism. An agnostic trend is gaining ground.

But this is only one example. There are no more taboos. Where
a puritanical prelate once opened a Catholic exhibition of 'decent'
bathing-suits, now an official report is clearing the way to aboli-
tion of moral censorship. Voices dare to protest the influence of
the Church on social activities, and to blame it for the woeful
state of education in the province. Clergy and laymen are res-
pectfully but firmly making public gestures of independence that
they would never have made ten years ago.

The revolution has, of course, affected the press, which used
to be characterized by scanty information and mediocre com-
mentary and style. In Montreal traditionally conformist papers
have found new spirit. *Le Devoir,* with its 50,000 readers, is no
longer fighting alone against systematic degeneration. In 1961-2,
the fleeting life of *Le Nouveau Journal,* directed by Jean-
Louis Gagnon (who would have been a 'communist' to Mr.
Duplessis), had great influence on new ideas and new style.
And the venerable and voluminous (260,000 copies) *La Presse*

acquired as editor-in-chief Gérard Pelletier (until 1965, when he won a seat in the federal Parliament). Pelletier was founder and leader of the little review *Cité libre,* which exposed the Duplessis régime with courageous clarity, despite attacks from the highest political and religious circles.

Government, for the first time in a long while, found itself face to face with public opinion capable of expressing itself, criticizing, remembering electoral promises, unmasking what some would like to keep modestly veiled. The free play of democracy is re-winning its rights; so much so that the CBC studios in Montreal are full of young producers who work for the future and refuse to venerate a past menaced as much by sclerosis as by Americanization. Premier Lesage, a Liberal, even seemed somewhat worried when he told me in June 1962 that he hoped the re-establishment of democracy in Quebec would take place in an orderly manner.

His team includes men who push him hard. Far from the least amazing thing in this supposedly conservative province is to hear talk of nationalization and socialism, while just across the international boundary lies the guardian of free enterprise.

In the strongly clerical province, the Catholic unions have secularized themselves (several years before France's C.F.T.C. became the C.F.D.T.), and have renamed themselves Confederation of National Trade Unions (C.N.T.U.). This change of name clearly demonstrates that the new winds blowing in the province of Quebec have gone beyond student, journalist, and Liberal circles – all of whom had scores to settle with Duplessis's conservatives – and reached all sectors of the population.

Order, authority, the hierarchy, religion, family, free enterprise – these were society's bywords in the days of Duplessis. Progress, liberty, justice, the common good, economic organization – these are the themes of today.

The reversals are not the work of the Liberals alone, for they have ridden the current more than they have created it. For a long time many young people lived on the fringe of society, ignored or suspect, the favourite red herring of anyone trying to win or to keep power. All along, they were waiting to strike. Writers, journalists, actors, professors, members of liberal professions, union men, businessmen: all have grown up in a country suffering from a grave lack of trained men, where people reach positions of command while still very young.

Paul Sauvé, who succeeded Duplessis as leader of the party, soon earned the nickname of 'Mister However'. His speeches all had the same theme: 'Until now,' he would say, 'the Union Nationale did (or thought) such-and-such; however . . . .' And he announced changes of policy that some thought audacious, even foolhardy, but that met the needs and hopes of a people who had been too long in tutelage.

The upheaval continued, and the Liberals rode to power on general discontent and a certain spirit of rebellion. They came at exactly the right moment; part of the Church hierarchy wanted to ease their control, laymen wanted to affirm their independence in temporal matters, unions demanded fuller participation in public life, several papers were trying to rise above mediocrity and the golden chains of the corrupt former régime, and a whole people realized their nationalism could no longer feed itself on speeches betrayed by facts.

The Union Nationale was the *parti bleu*, which, with a man like Duplessis in charge, could use government contracts to ruin an adversary – all under the cloak of free enterprise. He could ruin reputations just as efficiently with whispering campaigns. He held under his thumb businessmen, parishes, and prelates with favours he distributed just prior to each election. In the provincial legislature he could openly tell his opponents to be quiet. It was not, properly speaking, a reign of terror; in the words of a Liberal slogan, it was 'Blue fear'. The *rouges* have been in power since June 1960. Under the guidance of Jean Lesage they have set in motion a 'quiet revolution' which is pulling Quebec out of its old fear and nostalgia. The task is to save the future of French Canada; it is an immense undertaking.

The stakes in the end are simple enough; it is the conservative nationalism of Duplessis, deliberately tuned to the past, based on folklore, clericalism, and 'return to the land', against the dynamic nationalism of the Liberals, preoccupied with social problems, accepting industrialization and modern techniques. Nationalism remains the lever: the wish to use a new dynamism to protect a

French enclave of six million among 200 million English-speaking people who possess enormous economic power. Some of Jean Lesage's men attack the problem cautiously, others with the fiery strength of an ancient, courageous people suddenly finding itself rejuvenated. Some people question the orientation of this team. Some complain that they are keeping Quebec nationalism cooped up inside a larger loyalty to Canada; for them the only solution is secession, total independence for the State of Quebec. Others, better informed of the terrible things wrought by narrow nationalisms in Europe and more aware of the economic realities of the continent, fear that any nationalism is a breeding-ground for reactionaries, and look for the solution in a certain type of socialism.

But the most pressing task was to free Quebec from the heavy heritage of Maurice Duplessis. To do that, both men and attitudes had to change.

THE REIGN OF CORRUPTION. For twenty years the Duplessis régime had seriously debased the public service. Competence and talent were systematically excluded from power, and at any given moment political favouritism won out over the 'technical' solutions offered by experts; it was a triumph of mediocrity and lack of courage. In the government in Quebec highly-placed civil servants, administrators, and specialists see daily the ravages of the Union Nationale during its twenty years in power, from 1936 to 1939, and then from 1944 to 1960.

In June 1960, even before choosing his cabinet, Jean Lesage ordered the guards at the doors of the various ministries not to allow 'any package or bundle of documents of any sort' to leave the building, 'except the personal effects of the ministers'. The order was not purely melodramatic, for many people would have been very happy to see certain compromising documents disappear from view. But Mr. Lesage had the prudence – overdone, in the opinion of some of his friends – not to carry out a purge of the civil service. Even though new blood has entered administrative ranks, too many survivors of the old régime are still there, sometimes paralysing efforts at reform. However, being a civil servant is no longer disreputable. Worthy men are eager to work there.

The Liberal victory on June 2, 1960, was hard won. The Liberals won an absolute majority in the provincial legislature, jumping from 17 to 50 seats, while the Union Nationale fell from 61 to 44. But in several areas the strong-arm men bequeathed by Duplessis organized automobile races to carry off ballot-boxes in the best Chicago style. In Montreal-Laurier some twenty polling-stations were robbed by conservative henchmen. False representatives of Liberal candidates turned up at some stations to 'scrutinize' the counting. Counterfeit ballots, marked ahead of time with the name of the conservative candidate, could be slipped in.

The political climate seemed to demand a major purge. Not all those who voted Liberal looked forward to the great clean-up; some quite matter-of-factly awaited their own taste of patronage. For the political tradition in Quebec is, unfortunately, patronage. It chains private businesses, charitable works, and religious organizations to the party in power. When a contractor signed a contract with the provincial government for some public works programs, both sides knew that the price had been grossly inflated; the day after the election, the contractor would receive from the government a list of voters to whom he had to send cheques, which he did, in order to win more contracts.

The facts were made known largely through the press. In March 1962, *Le Magazine Maclean*[1] published, under the title 'Terror in the Suburbs', a major exposé of the activities of Léo Rémillard, habitual criminal and mayor of Ville Jacques Cartier. Although you need a spotless record to become a taxi-driver, no such standard is set for municipal candidates. Week after week newspapers published almost daily accounts of venal policemen being disciplined, of major and minor political-financial scandals, of elected members being threatened and prevented from taking their seats by Union Nationale strongmen. In the same article *Le Magazine Maclean* denounced 'the tacit complicity of citizens who don't vote' and 'government indecision'. The scope of the criminal activities and the courageous stand of Montreal newspapers finally forced the government in Quebec City to intervene;

[1]French-language sister to *Maclean's* Magazine.

Ville Jacques Cartier was at last placed under government control.

There are many other examples of changing ways in Quebec. But it is not enough to find honest policemen to stop adventurers from going gun in hand to carry off ballot-boxes. The most difficult task is still to cleanse the mores that give English Canadians an easy excuse for looking down on their French-speaking compatriots. The politicians of Ontario or Manitoba are not above reproach. But the political scandals that have burst on Canada have repeatedly highlighted French-Canadian names, spread them in headlines across the country, and strengthened a deep prejudice against French Canadians.

The favourite methods of the Duplessis régime had been denounced in 1956 by two Catholic priests, Fathers Dion and O'Neill, one a professor at Laval University and the other in the Petit Séminaire de Québec. Their text, published in the bulletin *Ad Usum Sacerdotum*, whose circulation is about 700 copies, would probably have caused little reaction if *Le Devoir*[1] had not reprinted it. From then on, the English-language press kept the question alive.

This article revealed the circumstances of the June 1956 electoral campaign which returned Duplessis to power with a comfortable majority of seventy-two seats out of ninety-three. The two priests described 'the outbreak of stupidity and immorality' in Quebec the day before the voting, and added, 'Perhaps never has our religious crisis been so clearly demonstrated.' According to their testimony, ballots had been priced quite highly in the electoral Stock Exchange:

> We have been told of several cases where voters not only have not refused to sell their vote, but actually have offered it themselves, in exchange for money or generous gifts. They were paid with roof repairs, the payment of hospital bills or maternity expenses, and promises of fat contracts, etc., not to mention the parade of refrigerators and television sets. In a certain working-class district, the voters showed their practicality; hundreds of pairs of shoes were exchanged for political convictions. On one little suburban street of some fifteen families, at least four sold their vote for a generous mess of pottage.

[1] *Le Devoir*, August 7, 1956.

Fathers Dion and O'Neill also denounced 'the use of religion' for political ends. In order to 'bring into action the defence mechanisms of the faithful', they wrote, the manipulators had denounced everywhere 'pseudo-enemies of religion'. Anti-communism was 'used with considerable success' thanks to 'low quality literature [which] found its way into the presbyteries and convents'. But, they added, 'there are some cases where, unfortunately, the motive for voting was less well-intentioned. There is every reason to believe that not only laymen were influenced by such gifts. Gifts to religious or charitable organizations and contributions to parish associations knew how to reach certain ecclesiastical souls.' Moreover, 'some priests entered quite directly into the fray.' One curé preached the virtues of a certain candidate from his pulpit, and even solicited votes door-to-door. Another said, 'Vote for whoever you wish, but when you have a good government, you should hang on to it.' But the prize goes to the one who, during his sermon, told his parishioners, 'Before going to vote, take a good look at our lovely new school.'

The electoral methods of the Union Nationale were well known. The significant fact is not that they were denounced by Fathers Dion and O'Neill, but that the denunciation was so long in coming. For the great majority of the population the article had impact, not because it revealed anything new about electoral methods, but because it dared to criticize the Union Nationale openly. This is why the two priests could remark, 'What ought to disturb us most is that so few people seem to be outraged by all this.'

This public indifference to political corruption was undoubtedly the result of the support given that system by the silence of the Catholic Church, considered as the guardian of morals. The clergy taught individual morality which, according to Fathers Dion and O'Neill, emphasized the sins of 'luxury, intemperance and blasphemy' while 'injustice, lying, collusion and lack of public spirit' were left discreetly in the shadows. True to this narrowly individualistic conception of morality, the Church never thought of denouncing scandals which some priests and religious institutions both supported and benefited from. Rare were the clergymen who dared to speak up, as, for example, did Father

Lavergne in 1935, from the pulpit of Notre Dame de Grâce:

> The régime lists with proud complacency its gifts to religious institutions, schools, shelters, hospitals. . . . These infamous gifts are a favorite means of forcing those who benefit to dance to the required tune. In an institution which I cannot name, but I know what I'm talking about, the superiors were forced to get rid of an excellent professor because he refused to kneel to the régime. . . .[1]

This system was at the heart of the political-clerical paternalism that held Quebec in mediocrity and stagnation, and ruled for twenty triumphant years alongside the obscurantism of Maurice Duplessis. But the régime being denounced by Father Lavergne in 1935 was Liberal, not Union Nationale. History somewhat tempers the optimism that arose after the death of Duplessis. In fact, scandals have blown up around some Liberal personalities since the disappearance of the Union Nationale 'Chief'. Men were not solely to blame; it was a whole concept of political life. The electoral 'machine', as in the United States, carried out its role, which was to win an election and not to advance democracy or to purify attitudes.

One and a half centuries ago the Quebec *Mercury* commented on the election of 1817, quoting a verse that it attributed to Shakespeare: 'Gold were as good as twenty orators.'

Duplessis was not an accident. He belonged to a line with a long pedigree. But the successors to the 'Chief' had neither his authority nor his experience in such delicate matters. Moreover, a reaction to all this was taking place in public opinion – a reaction influenced by young intellectuals who had often studied in foreign universities, by the pressure of young clergymen who saw the dangers of clericalism, by the action of several brave men who spoke out on television or wrote for the little reviews like *Cité libre,* and finally, by the new Liberal team that won by emphasizing the unemployment the conservatives could not handle, as well as the corruption of the Union Nationale itself.

The victors of 1960 could not have held power long in this new climate if they had fallen back on the old methods of their predecessors. They had no intention of destroying themselves

[1]Quoted by Marcel and Jean Jamelin in *Les Moeurs électorales dans le Québec de 1791 à nos jours,* Editions du Jour, Montreal.

by a return to corruption. But the significant fact is that, had they yielded to such temptation, they would have suffered the merciless criticism of the most active sectors of the population. By a slow transformation of attitudes, democratic contests had become possible. An important turn had been taken, and it had become politically dangerous to halt half-way.

Political corruption and gangster mentality ceased to dominate the electoral scene. But was Duplessis's other mainstay, clericalism, equally threatened?

THE CHURCH REJECTS THE MIDDLE AGES. The Catholic Church knew how to make material advantage out of its long association with a corrupt political system, advantage that may some day prove costly. But ecclesiastical society could no more escape the changes in Quebec than could civil society. The 'reconversion' of the Church was prepared by many different groups – Catholic Action groups, especially the student-level J.E.C.; Catholic unions, often rebellious against episcopal control and successful in dropping the religious terms from their names despite Church pressure; and the young clergy, receptive to European Catholic trends. Ten years before Vatican II, who would have believed that Cardinal Léger, Archbishop of Montreal, would distinguish himself in the Council and shock the conservative elements of the Roman Curia?

'Greetings, my city! You have made yourself beautiful to receive your prince . . . ,' he declared in 1950 when he was made archbishop. He came an authoritarian, much more a prince of the Church than a shepherd of souls. But time passed and when he addressed a laymen's group in 1961, he took quite another tone: 'The Church is a hierarchical community of free men, where dialogue is as much a duty as obedience.' He has often repeated this theme in public, inviting laymen to express themselves freely since they are responsible in their own domain. And he urges them to take initiative: 'Yesterday's formations are obsolete. The best-established institutions must adapt themselves if they are not to harm others or be destroyed themselves,' he said in June 1961.

The reaction to such speeches was predictable – indignation

among prelates who think they have a special gift for detecting heresy; confusion among men who for generations were accustomed to ask no questions and to make no decisions without first consulting the priest; but comfort and hope among the young clergy, the intellectuals, and the radicals who had had enough of a hierarchy sure of its own rightness, even though it was far removed from real problems. Cardinal Léger was probably the only prelate who prepared for his part in the Council by systematic consultation with his flock, so that he could appear in Rome not as the source and sole judge of immutable truth, but as the spokesman for the laymen and clergy of his diocese.

Even within the Church, something has changed. And, even though a courageous minority had long been pressing for the changes, once again it was the death of Maurice Duplessis that set them in motion. The same Duplessis who, talking about the bishops to whom he granted subsidies, boasted in the legislature of 'making them eat from my hand'.

It was not an empty boast. His very real power can be seen in the tragic case of Mgr. Charbonneau, whose dismissal on January 30, 1950, stunned the entire world.[1]

The mystery has not yet been completely unravelled. Mgr. Charbonneau became Archbishop of Montreal in August 1940. Ten years later, having won the affection and trust of his people, he was ordered to retire by the Vatican. Why? His views clashed with those of the nuncio, Mgr. Antoniutti, who later became nuncio in Madrid; he supported Catholic Action, which was in disfavour with certain other bishops; he involved himself in social conflict, particularly in the 1949 school-teachers' strike and the great strike of asbestos workers. 'We are more concerned with man than with money,' he said. He also dared to speak out for compulsory education, when generations of French Canadians had been moulded by the manuals of Mgr. Pâquet and Father Lortie, who considered that compulsory education was in conflict with the rights of parents and that it led straight to socialism.

One thing is clear: Mgr. Charbonneau was slandered at the Vatican by French and Canadian ultraclericals. Mgr. Courchesne,

[1]Cf. Renaude Lapointe, *L'Histoire bouleversante de Mgr Charbonneau*, Editions du Jour, Montreal 1962.

Archbishop of Rimouski, fired off a letter to Rome that found willing readers. The Montreal Archbishop was particularly suspect in the eyes of his Rimouski counterpart because he urged the secularization of co-operatives and Catholic unions, reforms that have since been made. The Vatican was flooded with attacks on Mgr. Charbonneau from Canadian bishops and from emissaries of Duplessis. *Cité Catholique,* which later established its international headquarters in Quebec, knew that it would find a sympathetic atmosphere there. The firm coalition of Canadian ultra-clericals, their supporters in Rome, and the Quebec government did its work. It fitted in with events in France, where the best theologians and the worker-priests were being silenced. Mgr. Charbonneau had to retire. He was exiled to a retreat house, where he died of grief several years later.

Even after the death of Duplessis and the replacement of Pius XII by John XXIII in Rome, the ultraclericals were still dangerous. Cardinal Léger was not spared their attacks. Now he was in a position to see the true value of their slanders. He found out who were the false friends, and he discovered the danger posed to society by excessive clericalism. The social structure of his diocese taught him that clericalism had no place in a society that was no longer solidly, homogeneously Catholic. Religious pluralism had won its place, and laymen had shown that they were ready to take on their responsibilities. Being 'prince' was increasingly less relevant.

But the Church in Quebec requires far-reaching reforms indeed. Before his disgrace Mgr. Charbonneau once chided the superior-general of a religious community for having too keen a sense of business. The reproach is still justified for most of the religious orders, many of which use their vast land holdings for speculative ends. Although Canadian Catholics have often shown their generosity, the methods used to collect such sums have sometimes approached thievery. The 'sounds of money around the altar' become particularly odious in such cases.

In December 1961 a scandal blew up about Spes, an organization that specialized in increasing parish revenues. It was then directing a campaign in one diocese expected to net $11 million. Other such agencies were at work in the same way, and apparently not all of them were perfectly respectable, for Cardinal Léger twice warned his priests about several of them.

Spes asked parishioners to contribute ten per cent of their earnings, and it used all possible methods to accomplish this goal. Some businessmen were bluntly told that their businesses would face serious reverses unless they came up with the required tithe. Parishioners were asked to fix the amount to be demanded of neighbours and friends. And Spes proclaimed, 'The old habit of anonymous donations profits no one but the hypocrite.' The organization even composed several rather bizarre prayers about money, and a profession of faith entitled 'Our credo': 'We believe that the silent gift of the past must be discouraged, for it has allowed many Catholics to hide their shamefully small contributions behind the mask of anonymity.' It was the direct negation of the Biblical precept, 'Therefore when thou doest thine alms, do not sound a trumpet before thee, as the hypocrites do in the synagogues and in the streets, that they may have glory of men. Verily I say unto you, They have their reward.'

Laymen have denounced such scandals; the reaction has begun. But the Church is still not free from the chains of money that have often made it the ally of conservative forces. And one can well ask how much reform is possible unless the Vatican radically modifies the rules about ownership of property by religious communities.

Other chains must be broken as well. Late in 1960 a smash best-seller burst on Quebec: *Les Insolences du Frère Untel* (The Impertinences of Brother Anonymous). More than 145,000 copies were sold in a few months. But Brother Anonymous did not remain anonymous very long, and the author, a teaching brother, was packed off to Rome. His superior was invited to reflect in peace and solitude, somewhere in France.

It does not really matter how insolent Frère Untel was, for the astounding success of the book, showed how many Quebec Catholics were ready to lash out at the all-enveloping conformity. The author's success was due simply to the fact that he had shouted aloud what so many were muttering under their breath. Did he deserve disciplinary measures for having denounced 'joual' (a type of patois named for its mispronunciation of 'cheval')? Or for having criticized a system of teaching that was in fact sadly deficient? Or for having allowed himself a few remarks about the clergy?

A good many young priests and members of religious orders read *Les Insolences* with delight. In an easy, if somewhat awkward, way the book destroyed an official image that no longer had anything to do with reality. It swept away dangerous shackles of conformity. Many Catholics, especially young ones, have left the Church because its image has become so unbearable.

The sermons to be heard in a good number of churches, including the cathedral in Montreal, reveal a sad weakness in doctrine, which urgent appeals to discipline cannot hide. Such sermons ignore the fact that, thirty years ago, Catholic Action formed an enlightened lay organization which is still asking the clergy to adopt a less authoritarian and less elementary attitude. But that would necessitate a reform at the Montreal Grand Seminary; and there, as far as many of the instructors are concerned, an appeal to intelligence is a sin.

Many prelates believe that Cardinal Léger went sadly astray when he renounced the old authoritarian attitudes. Historically, the clergy, which used to be the only élite, have played the major role in protecting the French-Canadian personality. But times have changed. With European and North American university educations, many laymen are now intellectually superior to the majority of young priests fresh from the seminaries. Clericalism no longer has any sociological necessity. Only nostalgia for the past can inspire part of the clergy and the episcopacy to carry on outmoded traditions. 'It would be futile,' warned Cardinal Léger, 'to want to live in some sort of illusory Middle Ages.'

The structures of the Middle Ages have disappeared, but the mentality still survives in too many areas. Industrialization and urbanization are forcing the Church to discard old attitudes. Slowly, it is trying to adapt. The extent to which it manages to change will determine how much of its structure will survive. French Canada no longer depends on clerical authoritarianism. Should the Church take too long in changing, it will steadily lose influence, something that is already happening among young intellectuals.

The clergy have made a major contribution to the strength of the 'French fact' over the centuries. The French Canadian finds in his language and his faith two reasons to struggle against the English-speaking and Protestant environment. But the efforts of the Church – and it has made errors – are no longer enough. Men have undertaken the political, economic, and social transformation of Quebec. The future of French Canada depends on the success of their efforts. Will the Church, by some irony of fate, play no part in this decisive task? The answer is up to the dynamic members of the clergy, the men who are part of the spirit of Vatican II and are working to modernize both the style and the content of the Church's teachings.

THE FAILINGS OF EDUCATION. Under the exclusive control of the Church, education was limited for too long a time to the humanities, while it scorned the sciences. The object was to produce lawyers and priests, not engineers. The graduates were scarcely prepared for the North American world of big business, finance, and commerce. The government of Jean Lesage has set in motion a major overhaul of the educational system. The reform must protect education from the influence of the Church. The scope of the task can only be measured in the light of what existed before. A few quotations from school books in use in Montreal on the eve of the reform[1] tell more about it than any learned exposé:

Problem:
'Jeannine prayed nine minutes at the tomb of Brother André, two minutes in the chapel, and ten minutes in the Basilica. How long did she pray altogether?'

Conjugation:
Conjugate orally in the simple-past tense:
'to be present at a burial'
'to decorate the tomb with flowers'
'to meditate on one's ultimate fate'

Recitation:
A 'poem' by Octave Crémazie:
'Bring this tribute of prayers and tears
So that at the terrible and fearful moment

[1]See Solange and Michel Chalvin, *Comment on abrutit nos enfants*, Editions du Jour, Montreal, 1962.

When the term of your life has come to an end,
Your name, repeated in the gratitude
Of those whose sufferings you have eased,
Will not be unknown when you arrive on high.'
Catechism:
'To receive baptism, we must repent our sins. . . .'
Spelling:
'Truly, only weak souls have shaking fingers and sorrowful hearts:
The man who passionately loves his country does not find it cold.'
or
'It is a good thing to see the convivial family supper where each
plate bears a little piece of the mother's heart.'

And to conclude, a question that seems to belong more in a
mathematics text than in a catechism: 'How many venial sins
equal one mortal sin?'

These gems were taken from texts officially approved by the
presiding school commission. The most surprising aspect is not
that teachers wrote and used such texts, for under the Duplessis
régime even the most alarmed parents merely grumbled under
their breath. The biggest surprise is that there was an editor in
Montreal courageous enough to publish such a collection of
stupidities; a few years earlier such daring would have brought
the full fury of the government and the Church down on his
head. And the success of the book showed public opinion existed
to support reforms in education.

Under the circumstances, British tradition came to the aid of
French Canada. This tradition, in a Confederation with an
English majority, had prevented Duplessis from venturing too
far into dictatorship. This same tradition offered the means of
putting the question to public opinion and of settling it; the
Lesage government set up a royal commission to study the entire
question and then to suggest reforms – a 'royal' commission because H. M. Queen Elizabeth II, in London, watches over her
faithful subjects in the Commonwealth.

The chairmanship of the Commission went to Mgr. Parent,
for it would be necessary to force the Catholic episcopacy to
suffer a major diminution of its powers. Though such men as
Cardinal Léger accepted the project, other bishops were firmly
opposed.

The Commission spent months travelling the province, recording the speeches and briefs of both individuals and groups – teachers' groups, groups of parents of school children, groups of administrators, of clergymen, etc. The debates and speeches were given wide coverage in the press. Such a Commission has wide-ranging powers; it can even imprison anyone refusing to obey its summons to a meeting. The final decisions are up to the Quebec government; but for political reasons, it would never dare ignore the findings of a Commission that it itself had appointed.

The voluminous report of the Parent Commission was published in 1964-5. It examined every aspect of teaching: organization, financing, curricula, teacher qualifications. A preliminary report released in the autumn of 1962 recommended the creation of a ministry of education, something the Church had always opposed. The ministry was created, with its first head Paul Gérin-Lajoie, assisted by a council. Although the episcopacy has only a consultative voice on the council, it still wields the true power in education.

The reform came into effect in the autumn of 1965. It eliminates various anomalies in the academic structure, but above all, it sets new standards for teachers and textbooks. Most religious communities had their own Normal schools, no matter how mediocre, for the preparation of teachers. Now every teacher must have a university diploma, which is subject to provincial control. Only books approved by the Minister of Education may be used. Since 1965 Quebec and France have been working together to develop both teachers and textbooks.

The educational system has long held back the evolution of Quebec; its teachings were not responsive to the needs of the twentieth century. The full effects of the reform will not be felt for several years yet, but the most crucial part was undoubtedly the overcoming of inertia.

As a corollary – and a by no means negligible one – the reform in teaching will turn the publishing world topsy-turvy. Education is under governmental subsidy, and Quebec editors depend largely on their school publications. These include not only books but also magazines designed for the schoolroom, such as the monthly *L'Elève,* which has a circulation of 520,000 and a standard as low as the books quoted above. Afraid of losing their school business, the editors took care not to publish novels, essays, or poetry that might displease the Church or Premier Duplessis. Thus the government and the episcopacy had effective control of publishing.

And so, the complete reshaping of the educational system will do more than bring about better instruction for students. It will break open the barriers to free circulation of ideas.

At the same time, Quebec is moving toward the creation of its first non-confessional schools, which will not be under the control of either Catholic or Protestant churches. Just prior to the reform Quebec had 990,000 students in Catholic elementary and secondary schools and 116,000 in Protestant. Three Catholic universities accounted for 43,000 students, three Protestant ones for 25,000.[1] The people who wanted a non-confessional education had nowhere to go. But, as Mr. Robert Elie, cultural counsellor with the Quebec Delegation in Paris, said, 'the French Canadian community is . . . of a pluralist nature. Though the majority are Catholic, there are also Protestants, Jews, and Orthodox Christians, as well as men and women who follow no religion. . . . A strictly confessional education is not suitable to this pluralist society which, moreover, wishes to democratize itself.' A lay movement was founded in Montreal in 1961, and, explained Mr. Elie, 'I belong to this movement more because I am Catholic than because I am democratic.'

There is no doubt that strictly confessional education has harmed the Church. The atheists of today were formed in Catholic schools. Now they demand that their children be spared such a religious education. Moreover, many of them no longer accept the fact that they cannot marry without being Catholic, since the Church controls the registration of marriages as it did in France before the Revolution.

The Church will be better off for losing its privileges that are no longer justified. And it seems that the archbishopric of Montreal saw the matter in just this light.

But indignant voices rose on every side: 'They want to take

[1] Cf. *Annuaire statistique,* pages 227 and 237.

the crucifix out of our schools!' Such protests ignore the fact that the present reforms are only making fact out of the theoretical separation of Church and State that became law in 1852-4. The various denominations would be well-advised to be the first to ask for revision of articles 44 and 129 of the Civil Code. These two articles make it the churches' responsibility to keep marriage registers and to celebrate marriages. Such changes would benefit the churches (Catholic and Protestant) and would help to prevent a serious rift in the French-speaking community on the subject of marriage and divorce.

Such conflicts may not be far off. When the Mouvement Laïque du Québec established contact with the Ligue de l'Enseignement in France, the editor of *Le Devoir*[1] wrote a vehement editorial on the subject. He asked France to keep its ultraclericals from Cité Catholique at home . . . and its Ligue de l'Enseignement laymen as well. Using a lovely little Canadianism, he requested Frenchmen to keep their quarrels at home and not 'enfirouâper' Canada with them. He added a footnote explaining the verb: 'A Canadian expression which can mean anything, including "to cover with sh . . " .'

The educational changes have made spirits bubble over. University students and intellectuals, who used to live in an ivory tower, have since the Second World War become aware of international trends in thought. Their diplomas are no longer only Canadian, but French, English, and American as well. They were stifled during Duplessis's era when the mere fact that an idea came from somewhere else made it anti-national and subversive. Now they breathe more freely. The Reverend Father Lévesque had to wage a Homeric battle to create a faculty of social sciences at Laval University, where the narrow-minded nationalistic arguments are being shot full of holes. Now the intellectuals can express themselves, and their advice is even formally solicited.

More and more young Quebec writers have their books published in Paris, and several French publishing-houses have brought out joint editions with Canadian publishers. Painters have broken with the folkloric tradition and have found a universal language, so much so that their canvases can be found in

[1]*Le Devoir,* May 30, 1962.

galleries on the Left Bank. Plays by Pirandello, Ionesco, and Brecht are performed in Montreal, and the young French-Canadian theatre has taken enormous strides in the past ten years. Quebec singers have known major successes in Paris. Quebec is losing the provincialism that some Frenchmen used to disparage, a reaction that annoyed and humiliated French Canadians. Like the St. Lawrence, with its gulf open to the world, the people of the St. Lawrence have now turned their faces to the world. One of the more significant manifestations of Quebec's new involvement in the entire world took place in 1961 when the first international conference of French-language universities took place, not in Paris, but in Montreal.

Quebec cut its ties with the outside world in order to safeguard its distinctive ways. But in fact, the long isolation merely perverted or destroyed them. Suddenly Quebec realized the impurity of its language and set up a remedial Office of the French language. It can no longer live on the past, and its efforts to change and to meet the future occasionally bring on a sort of vertigo, a kind of drunkenness. The calm of yesterday's sleepy life allowed it to slide, without any awkward questions, into petty tomorrows. The torpor, which seemed to give it so much pleasure, in fact condemned it to the Anglo-Saxon world, which looked on it condescendingly as a pleasant little anachronism.

For many, the awakening was brutal, and they were the very first to demand radical solutions: Quebec must be saved, which meant the transformation of all its internal structures. But did it not also mean reconsidering the whole question of being part of the Canadian Confederation? The people who argued this question most passionately were often young people who had not known the Duplessis régime, or older ones who refused to admit that their own indifference and silence had made them accomplices in a situation that threatened to destroy French Canada. They threw themselves into the future, refusing any examination of the recent past which would have afforded plenty of nourishment for an unbearable guilt complex. For it was neither the English nor the Americans who had imposed on them antiquated and mediocre schooling, an agricultural economy, and a reactionary, corrupt political apparatus. They chose these things them-

selves, through blindness, ignorance, or laziness. They had the
ballot; they were free to set the quiet revolution in motion fifty
years ago. But facing the facts would be unbearable. And so they
avoid any examination of themselves or their fathers. The 'English' are there, the perfect scapegoat for all of Quebec's problems.

But are the 'English' simply a scapecoat? Can they wash their
hands of any responsibility for the progressive deterioration of
the situation in Quebec? If Quebeckers are 'second-class citizens', is it entirely their own fault? The 'English' claim it is,
but they cannot get off so easily. And so English good conscience
meets Quebec's uneasy conscience, and separatism flourishes in
the resulting lack of understanding. And separatism has no
trouble finding abundant examples of solid economic, political,
cultural, and judicial grievances against the English.

THE BIRTH OF SEPARATISM. Anglo-American capitalism met
only feeble resistance in Quebec, so Anglo-Americans naturally
took over the administrative positions, allowing French Canadians to fill the rest. When the day of awakening came, this was
a major source of resentment. Five vice-presidents sat in their
sleek board-room one day in 1961, talking business and drinking
rye. English was the mother tongue for four of them, French for
one. 'The legitimate aspiration of every vice-president,' said the
French Canadian, 'is to become president. One of us cannot
realize that ambition; that one is me, for I am French
Canadian.'

This anecdote was whispered all around Montreal, and English Canadians began to wonder. One of them asked a French-
Canadian friend to explain to him the bases of French-Canadian
nationalism. After a long and hotly disputed evening, he slammed
the door on his friend with a muttered 'After all, we beat the
French in 1759. If Quebec wants to try secession, let her remem-
ber how the United States treated the South in 1861-5.'

How embittered are the relationships between the two groups?
The French Canadians present their long list of grievances: their
economy is dominated by Anglo-American capital; the 'damned
English' control the federal government, with a couple of French
names thrown in; the leaders of both major parties, John Diefen-

baker and Lester Pearson, are English; Quebec supports English-language schools, but outside their own province French Canadians very rarely find any French-language schools; they have had to fight a dozen years for bilingual cheques in the banks; French Canadians are tired of being treated like a minority; they cannot feel at home in Ontario or Saskatchewan. If Quebec, which is 13 per cent English, is bilingual, why is New Brunswick, which is more than 35 per cent French, unilingual?

English Canadians, who admit that Italian immigration is something of a problem (Italians head the list of immigrants with an average 7,500 a year for the province of Quebec alone), realized a little too late that the French-Canadian minority can create even more difficult problems. They suddenly woke up when a book written by a separatist leader, Marcel Chaput, sold 35,000 copies in a few months.

The whole business took on new importance in 1961 when Mr. Chaput, leader of the Rassemblement pour l'Indépendance Nationale (R.I.N.), lost his job with the federal government because, according to his superiors, he took time off to give a public conference. His dismissal meant unhoped-for publicity for the R.I.N. Accusations were hurled about, and the movement gained members, carefully organized by city and district. Little by little, recruiting has been falling off. Nevertheless, people of all social classes who are not actually members of the R.I.N. still feel a very real sympathy for its beliefs. And this is not a surprising attitude for a linguistic and ethnic minority to take when they are daily treated like poor relations.

What are the aims of the R.I.N. and how does the movement hope to achieve them? I got my answer in the spring of 1962 from one of its most brilliant leaders, André d'Allemagne. This man is young, intelligent, and completely devoid of any sense of apostolic mission. His very calmness lent weight to his words, words that a messianic fervour would have made suspect.

'Canada is an artificial country,' he said, 'separated from the United States by an artificial border that stretches for thousands of miles from coast to coast. Its population is strung out along this border, so that a resident of British Columbia or Alberta finds it more natural to do business with his American neighbour

DISTRIBUTION OF POPULATION

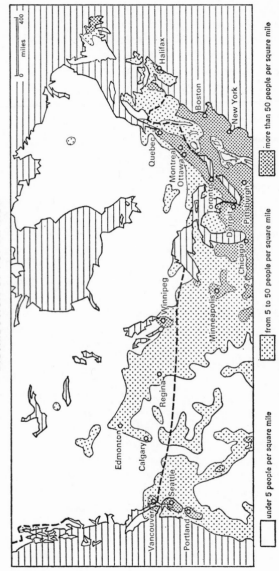

Geography itself is a challenge to the Canadian nation. From Vancouver to St. John's, Newfoundland, more than eighteen million people are massed along a 4,000-mile border, although their country is eighteen times larger than France. 'Canada is an artificial country' is the separatist conclusion.

under 5 people per square mile

from 5 to 50 people per square mile

more than 50 people per square mile

than with far-off provinces like Quebec or Nova Scotia, let alone Newfoundland. To create an artificial unity in the country, they've installed a central government in Ottawa, and built roads and railways the length of the boundary.'

His comments are added to my very long conversations with the many young people who amuse themselves in gloomy introspection, complaining of their submersion in everything that comes from the United States and of belonging to a country which, they claim, 'doesn't exist'. They scrutinize their history to find all the things that distinguish them as French Canadians from the Anglo-Saxons who surround them. They believe they can only discover their identity in the traditions of the past, and they are panic-stricken that they have lost ground. 'What a lamentable situation is that of this poor French-Canadian people who, after four centuries of history, are still asking themselves if they're a nation,' wrote Marcel Chaput.[1]

There are French Canadians, especially in a city like Montreal, who feel they have lost the game and have no future but integration with the United States. The separatists answer this with the example of Louisiana, which drowned in the American environment and became an English-language state. Separatists know that demography is against them, for immigration favours the English provinces. French Canadians were 29 per cent of the 1951 population of Canada, but if present trends continue, their percentage will shrink to 20 per cent by the year 2000. They hate being a minority, but are becoming more and more a minority every day. Thus, the Confederation pact that ties them to the central power seems the very instrument of their own disappearance. They wish to break this pact by secession.

Their plans should not be taken lightly, for they are founded on realities that must be settled one way or another. At the heart of their movement is the fact that Quebec pays $2 billion a year in federal taxes, but gets back only 25 per cent of it. According to the Tremblay Report of 1956, the tax on development of Quebec's forests brings $100 million a year to Ottawa, but only $15 million to the province. The tax on mining is distributed in the ratio of four to one, favouring Ottawa. Ontario, with only a

[1]*Pourquoi je suis séparatiste,* op. cit.

slightly larger population, has 10,467 miles of railway while Quebec has 5,096. Ontario is industrializing more rapidly than Quebec, unemployment is usually lower in Ontario, and the average wage per citizen is rising faster. Quebec is thus handing over an excessive share of its resources to a Confederation that is not protecting its interests.

All this, according to the separatists, is Ottawa's fault. And they praise the example of Israel, urging their compatriots to build, doggedly, a proud and free nation. If Togo and Nicaragua, both smaller and poorer, have seats in the U.N., why not an independent State of Quebec? And if Cuba, they add, can defy Washington, why should we fear Ottawa? Marcel Chaput intends to bring back to Quebec that $2 billion a year in tax revenues, to nationalize key industries, to encourage manufacturing industries (and there are too few of them), to diversify sources of foreign capital in order to avoid dependence on the United States, etc. He insists: 'We do not want to correct injustices; we want to get rid of our minority status.'

Fine, say their adversaries, you'll isolate yourselves on the continent! And the answer is ready, 'Is it not an even worse isolation when, despite their membership in a world community of twenty-five French-speaking countries with 150 million inhabitants, one French Canadian in two cannot earn his living without leaving his mother tongue behind each morning? When French Canadians cannot enrol in the army of their own country, supposedly bilingual, without giving up their distinctive personality? When they cannot reach the top positions in industry or the civil service without forgetting for eight hours a day that they are French?'

But how do the separatists hope to reach their goals?

'We are not,' one of their leaders told me, 'a political party. Rightists, leftists, everyone can be a separatist, for that is the basis of our unity. So our objective is to elect a separatist government in Quebec that will turn to Ottawa and say, "We are leaving Confederation." Then the federal government will have to take a stand. Negotiations will start. We will not turn over federal taxes. If the negotiations don't work out, we will cut the country in two, separating the West from the Maritime Provinces.

Furthermore, don't forget that we will control the St. Lawrence Seaway. And that affects the United States as well. In short, we will have enough ways to make ourselves heard. A State of Quebec could collaborate with the government at Ottawa on terms decided by mutual consent. At present, we have to accept terms that were imposed on us.'

Such a process will necessarily take a long time. R.I.N. leaders realize this. They hope their arguments will convince a majority of French Canadians that they will never win respect within Confederation and that their only hope is to leave it. A gloomier economic situation and an increase in unemployment would strip from Canadians the illusion that they participate in the high North American standard of living, and would thus favour the separatist cause.

Nobody who listens to them could doubt that they intend to pursue their beliefs to the very end. And that is precisely what bothers English Canadians, and forces them to reopen a dossier they have too long neglected. Their past indifference to the French-speaking minority has made that minority extremely sensitive. The only possible answer to separatism is to allow French Canada its rightful position. But progress has been slight.

Separatists stumble against one serious obstacle after another. They cannot avoid the fact that French Canadians themselves have not always done their utmost to make their own place in the sun. Their nationalism has long been negative, anti-English, and ignorant of how to defend its own interests. Their nationalism was for centuries the workhorse of conservative forces when it should have been winning new ground. It has been defensive, not progressive. Their schooling, grounded in the humanities, has ignored the industrial age and the technical branches of knowledge. Yet economic power is the basis of political power. Too few French Canadians have had the ability or the desire to carry Quebec's voice to Ottawa by entering the federal administration.

At least the R.I.N. is facing up squarely to a real problem. Yet its program is simply not precise enough, especially in economic matters. At the same time, the Liberal government of Jean Lesage in Quebec is working hard to develop the economy of the province, and each concrete success in this field weakens the separatist argument.

This does not mean that the Lesage team is not working for a revised Confederation that will take account of the legitimate aspirations of French Canada. For though the inadequacies of the present pact may not condemn Canada to death, they do deprive it of its greatest potential: a working coexistence of two cultures that enriches both.

Yet the fact remains that in the past Quebec has not used its political power and economic resources to its own advantage within Confederation. Quebec has handled its affairs poorly. The Lesage government is trying to correct this. And that is where everything must start, for the soil and the subsoil of Quebec are immensely rich.

'LET US CONTROL OUR INDUSTRY'. 'Eighty-five per cent of the population of Quebec speaks French, but eighty-five per cent of our key industries are controlled by American or English capital.' The words are central to the thinking of René Lévesque, provincial Minister of Natural Resources. As a recent change, all correspondence of the ministry is carried on in French, unless a particular business requests that it be in English. In such a case, the company receives a reply expressing great surprise that they have no personnel competent in French. Total inability to cope with the French will mean that the correspondence will take place in English. But the firm will have been warned that it had better make serious efforts to acquire French-language staff.

A healthy reaction has been going on since 1960 against the Americanization of the language and the economy, not out of any wave of nationalism, but because the urgent problems of the day demand it. Unemployment in Quebec fluctuates between 10 and 12 per cent of the work force, sometimes reaching 15 per cent. The situation is quite literally intolerable, especially when compared with the province of Ontario, where the unemployment rate is only 6 per cent. *Per capita* income is more than $2,000 a year in Ontario but only $1,059 in Quebec, or 87 per cent of the national average. The labour force has shown a tendency to head out to the richer provinces or south to the

United States. Moreover, unemployment insurance payments impose a heavy burden on the general public.

The paradox is that Quebec has such an abundance of natural resources. It ranks high on the world scale in the production of wood, wood pulp and paper, iron, precious metals, and asbestos. Its enormous hydro-electric resources have led to the installation at Arvida of one of the world's principal aluminum centres. Yet Quebec shows many of the characteristics of an underdeveloped province: it exports raw materials and semi-finished products, and it must import a great many finished products. One of the prime aims is to develop manufacturing in Quebec. Plain common sense demands it. The primary materials are there, so are the workers. Europe can supply the skilled technicians as well as eventual financial help. The only thing still lacking is the desire to progress.

On this industrialization depends the entire future of Quebec. The Lesage government has undertaken the reorganization of education, the raising of its standards to meet the needs of today's world. But all efforts to save the French culture are doomed to failure if the economy of the province does not develop quickly. The task cannot be postponed; it is essential to create full employment in order to keep the necessary working force in Quebec, to develop economic potential to the maximum, and to build resources for the financing of activities that will assure the growth of French Canada. In order to preserve and develop its moral and intellectual patrimony, Quebec must exploit its economic potential to its utmost.

With 75 of the 265 members in the House of Commons, Quebec has a significant political weight in Ottawa. This can be strengthened by sending first-class men to the federal capital. But Quebec must also strengthen its position in the economic life of the country. To do that, it must begin to process raw materials within the province instead of exporting them.

The Ungava region in northern Quebec has rich deposits of iron. But this ore is sent from Quebec to Pittsburgh. The Lesage government has given French experts the task of studying the possibilities of a Quebec steel industry. With the necessary capital already at hand, the government has signed agreements to assure

European technical help, so that Quebec will have its own blast furnaces and rolling mills in a few years.

Renault and Peugeot have signed an agreement with the provincial government to set up an assembly plant for automobiles. Now the government is looking for ways to export fewer ingots

THE PRINCIPAL MINERAL RESOURCES OF QUEBEC

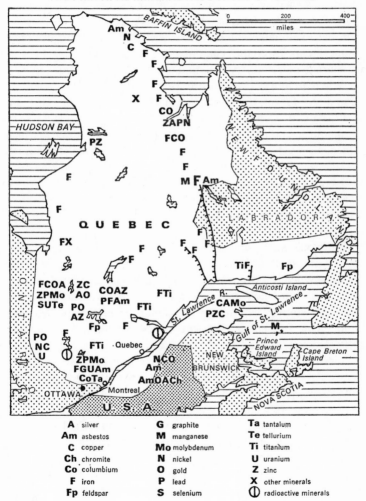

A	silver	G	graphite	Ta	tantalum
Am	asbestos	M	manganese	Te	tellurium
C	copper	Mo	molybdenum	Ti	titanium
Ch	chromite	N	nickel	U	uranium
Co	columbium	O	gold	Z	zinc
F	iron	P	lead	X	other minerals
Fp	feldspar	S	selenium	⊕	radioactive minerals

of aluminum and more aluminum products, less pulpwood and more paper. Rare metals also offer interesting possibilities which, until the present, have not been sufficiently explored. Since each province is responsible for its own natural resources, Quebec has full constitutional rights to reorganize the exploitation of its resources so as to benefit the province more and English and American companies less. The government cannot alter the concessions signed away by Premier Duplessis to an American company for iron-ore rights in Ungava. But it can introduce new rules for the exploitation of Quebec's vast forests. It can use such inducements as credit, guarantees, and favourable tax laws to encourage new industry based on Quebec's rich mineral deposits.

When it looked as if Great Britain was about to enter the Common Market, certain circles in Quebec were noticeably uneasy; without Commonwealth preferences there would be considerable uncertainty about the possible markets toward which Quebec's production should be oriented. The situation seemed to bear out a favourite separatist argument: only Commonwealth ties keep Canada from being completely absorbed by the United States, and Britain's entry into the Common Market would force Quebec to announce its independence as a sheer matter of survival.

But would secession save French Canada? Some adversaries of the separatist thesis believe an independent Quebec would never be economically viable. It is a doubtful argument; much poorer countries than Quebec are managing. Moreover, Quebec's great natural resources can attract the capital necessary for their development. But an independent Quebec would still be on the very doorstep of the United States. Independent or not, it would still have to fight hard against the influence of its powerful neighbour. And the other provinces, also dominated by American enterprise, are discovering that they must fight the same battle. In fact, Quebec's choice is between resisting alone, or resisting in the company of the other provinces within Confederation. Myths must be seen as such. Political independence has never guaranteed immunity from neo-colonialism, from economic imperialism. Many young countries have learned this the hard way. Quebec can, if it wishes, try, but it must do so without any illusions. Decades ago Quebec could have exploited Ungava iron ore to its own profit, nationalized electricity, and created a fund to encourage industry. It did not – not because Confederation prevented it, but because Quebec, in full sovereignty, chose to elect governments with antiquated ideas in the field of economics. With or without political independence, within Confederation as it exists at present or as it could be, the government of Quebec must develop its economic potential and take advantage of its resources.

It is an old story. At the beginning of this century, Mgr. Pâquet said, in the course of an important speech:

> Our mission is less to control business than to stir up ideas; it has less to do with lighting the furnaces of the factories than with kindling from afar the luminous hearth of religion and of thought. . . . Leave this feverish mercantilism and coarse animalism, which rivets one to material things, to other less sensitive nations. . . . While our rivals lay claim to . . . the supremacy of industry and finance, we aspire above all to the honour of doctrine and the laurels of the apostleship. . . .

The Church spread this attitude, encouraging the mystique of a return to the land, while people were in fact streaming from the countryside to the town, and teaching the virtues of artisanship, while mass production was being born. The 'luminous hearth of religion and of thought', as it appeared in Quebec, may have delighted Mgr. Pâquet, but it did not delight his compatriots or the rest of the world. Today's Quebec, no 'less sensitive', wants to light 'the furnaces of the factories' itself. And perhaps it is to avoid sullying the 'laurels of the apostleship' that Quebec must 'control business', if it does not want to fall completely to those who now run its economy. In the United States the first wave of pioneers went out across desert and mountain to conquer the land; the second built great industrial empires which today support the power of the country. French Canadians, on the contrary, explored the country from one end to the other and then shut themselves up in shops and family enterprises. Perhaps it is the result of military defeat, but there is a trace of the 'peasant' in their make-up, encouraged by a priesthood which is itself peasant-like in its attitude and its faith in the virtues of the soil.

So when industry and finance spread and ramified, it was with foreign capital. Voices repeatedly – and vainly – urged French Canadians to become more active in the economic sphere. They aroused nationalist emotions, but they did not manage to arouse daring industrial or financial activity.

In Quebec, as elsewhere, the War brought great upheavals. From 1940 to 1945, and during the Korean War as well, factories (aircraft, for example) sprang up around Montreal. They were American; their future depended on decisions made in Washington with very little concern for Canadian interests. The end of the Korean War brought a sharp rise in the level of unemployment from an average of 58,000 in 1953 to 164,000 in 1960. But by 1960 total personal income had increased by 118.3 per cent over 1949. French Canadians could believe in their prosperity, false comfort could lull them to sleep. They were not masters of their own economy; others decided in their name their degree of well-being or poverty. But this did not decrease their nationalism. They could, as Mgr. Pâquet had done earlier, look disdainfully upon those whom 'feverish mercantilism' had 'riveted to material things' – but they still obeyed their orders. Moreover, Americanization had penetrated their culture via the press, television, and the movies. They continued to 'have ideas', but the ideas were less and less their own, more and more those of their neighbours. Nationalism became a subject for abstract debate while economic subjugation increased. Religious teachers in the *collèges classiques* taught the humanities quite well, but American status symbols were the daily criteria applied to their culture.

But now one hears government speeches whose hallmark is the appeal that went unanswered at the turn of the century, 'Let us control our industry!' A conservative government like that of Premier Duplessis was largely responsible for American control of Quebec's economy, but made full use of demagogic nationalism as a campaign tool. Hostile to the 'English' both in England and in Canada, it opened all the doors to the Americans. Government speeches, though completely hollow, hid this deception by flattering traditional emotions. The Liberals who have governed Quebec since 1960 have not let their rivals forget it. Although they back off from any hint of chauvinism, they are serving

French-Canadian interests much better than did their predecessors.

Maurice Tremblay remarked quite rightly that in his opinion socialism would be 'the only completely logical nationalist attitude.'[1] His Liberal friends, who reject the old Conservative nationalism, are spontaneously orienting themselves toward certain innovations which are exciting but frightening when they seem to lead in a socialist direction. This is the psychological complexity of a people for whom words, long used with passion and inaccuracy in debate, have been twisted out of their true meaning.

While others carry on theoretical debates about French-Canadian nationalism and separatism, the Lesage government concerns itself with the Quebec economy. The first test was the nationalization of electricity. The idea brought on storms of outrage, as if hydro had not already been nationalized for half a century in Ontario and for several years in British Columbia. But Quebeckers, unaccustomed to taking decisive steps in economic matters, were frightened by their own audacity. How could they have thought up such an ambitious project? 'I won't jump in without testing the temperature of the water,' Mr. Lesage told me, while his Minister of Natural Resources, René Lévesque, protested that the temperature of the water was already well known. He wanted to get on with it and threatened to leave the party if it hesitated. It was a powerful threat, for the Liberal leaders had urged him to join their party precisely because of his enormous personal following.

Nationalization of electricity in this water-rich province would make possible a great deal of new industry. If they failed, the Liberals would have shown their inability to handle the economic problems that their American neighbour had made particularly urgent.

Finally, Mr. Lesage decided that the voters should have a say in it. He dissolved Parliament in November 1962 and called an election for November 14. Nationalization of electricity was a major issue, though not the only one. The ballot-boxes made the

---

[1] Article in J. C. Falardeau (ed.), *Essais sur le Québec contemporain*, Université Laval, Québec, 1953.

verdict clear; the Liberals moved from 54 to 63 seats, taking 9 away from the Union Nationale, which fell to 31 (one Independent was re-elected). With two-thirds of the provincial legislature in his hands, Mr. Lesage knew he could go ahead. Eleven private companies were nationalized a few months later, giving the province direct control of over nine million kilowatts of power. Not satisfied to have more harnessed energy than any other Canadian province, Quebec set up in Manicouagan a new hydro-electric complex with a capacity of six million kilowatts. Since provincial agencies are not subject to federal taxation, nationalization brought back to Quebec the $15 million in taxes that the private companies had been paying to Ottawa every year.

Nationalization was an important step for Quebec in several ways. Left to private initiative, the energy sources were badly distributed geographically, set up without any concern for regional needs. Now it is possible to distribute them across the province according to a general plan for economic development. Moreover, since Quebec had competent personnel in this field, it proved to English Canadians – and to itself – that it was capable of managing its own natural resources. It broke with the habits of the past, opening the way to other such initiatives, all of which would have been forbidden twenty years ago as 'socialist'. Finally, since the nationalized companies had been paid compensation, there was no panic among investors.

Other sectors of economic activity considered as public services – telephones, for example – are still in private hands, and reap huge profits for their owners. Their nationalization would give the government working funds which could be used for other development programs.

The Lesage team has created the Société Générale de Financement (S.G.F.), supported by government credit, private savings (Caisses Populaires), and private capital. By giving guarantees or by supplying funds, the S.G.F. has facilitated the opening of several industrial programs, which are either entirely Canadian or joint Canadian-European ventures. The S.G.F. has drawn to Quebec the Banque de Paris et des Pays-Bas, the Compagnie Générale d'Electricité, Peugeot and Renault, a French chemical company, and so on. S.G.F., moreover, has invested $25 million in Sidbec, the steel mill that is now being set up.[1] Besides its participation in Sidbec, S.G.F. had invested $9 million in 1965 – $6.4 million for the encouragement of existing enterprises (heavy machinery, heating appliances, food products, paper, synthetic fibres), and $2.6 million for the founding of six new enterprises (furniture factories, fertilizer, automobiles). S.G.F.'s participation ranges from 1.8 per cent of the capital to 100 per cent.

The director of the S.G.F., Gérard Filion, defined his objectives this way:

> In the past, we were not 'masters in our own house' because almost all the economic decisions were made outside Quebec and because the state had no way to control the economic activity in its territory. Thus the dominated economy that we have inherited. To reverse the situation we must have the economic decisions made in Quebec and the state must have the means to plan the economy. This presupposes a certain amount of control.

The Lesage government is working simultaneously toward 'recapturing' sectors of the Quebec economy that are under American or English control, and toward the founding of new economic activities. The object is to produce as much as possible inside Quebec, rather than to export raw materials and buy finished products.

Quebec shook off the politico-clerical paternalism of the Duplessis régime and set out on its quiet revolution. A new spirit had entered the political game. The Church is gaining new vigour. Education is adapting to the scientific and technological needs of the world. Economic initiatives to encourage the exploitation of Quebec's resources for its own advantage have been taken. Ideas are cropping up everywhere. A page has been turned. Quebec has renounced its bucolic myths, its touching anachronisms, its deceptive loyalties, and is at last emerging from the past.

A change in political power or a Liberal decline into bour-

---

[1]Sidbec will have $225 million invested in it: S.G.F., $25 million; public shares, $10 million; public bonds, $165 million; credit on equipment, $25 million. The enterprise will employ 2,000 people.

geois attitudes could slow the revolution but not reverse it. Any return to the past seems impossible. With a higher rate of growth the process of industrialization, which first became noticeable after the Second World War, has caused a significant growth in urban population. This urban population, influenced by the unions, by a lively Catholic Action movement, and by better education, has had a strong influence on the new climate of Quebec. Naturally, the rural areas lag behind the urban centres. Although an agricultural crisis is a factor for change, the old peasant individualism is, in Quebec as elsewhere, the best ally of conservatism. The rural areas, moreover, usually have the poorest schools, the most authoritarian clergy, and the least impressive newspapers, and thus are the last to be influenced by new trends from Montreal or Quebec City.

Population Growth in Quebec

Year	Total	Urban Population		Rural Population	
1871	1,191,516	271,851	22 %	919,665	78 %
1911	2,006,000	967,000	48 %	1,039,000	52 %
1921	2,361,000	1,323,000	56 %	1,038,000	44 %
1931	2,875,000	1,814,000	63 %	1,061,000	37 %
1941	3,332,000	2,110,000	63 %	1,222,000	37 %
1951	4,055,000	2,715,000	67 %	1,340,000	33 %
1961	5,259,211	3,906,404	74 %	1,352,807	26 %

Since 1871 the population of the province of Quebec has almost quadrupled. The rural population has risen by only 50 per cent, however, while the urban has increased fifteen-fold. Electoral boundaries have not been changed and thus the citizens most open to new ideas are at a political disadvantage. A new distribution of parliamentary seats is absolutely necessary if the government is to have the vitality to meet its problems.

But the county boundaries (which are also electoral boundaries) have not been redrawn, even though industrialization and urbanization mean most people now live in the cities. In 1871, the province of Quebec had 271,851 urban residents and 919,665 rural dwellers. By 1914 the two groups were equal. But the census of 1961 showed 3,906,404 urban against 1,352,807 rural, or 74 per cent to 26 per cent.[1] The electoral map, a very oddly drawn document, still gives the rural areas predominance in the provincial legislature. Montreal, for example, has 40 per cent of the voting population of the province, yet elects less than 20 per cent of the members of the provincial Parliament. The Liberals find their strongest support in the cities, and the antiquated electoral map works to their disadvantage.

Supporters of Mr. Lesage promised a redistribution of seats in line with new demographic and economic realities. Yet after several years in power, they still have not touched the problem. Are they afraid of injuring certain interests? If the Liberal party wants to consolidate and accelerate the progress it has already set in motion, it must give due parliamentary representation to the largest groups of the population, for these same groups are also the most aware of current problems, the most dynamic, the most ready to adopt daring solutions.

[1]Cf. *Annuaire statistique.*

The Debate

Will new political and economic strength in Quebec cut the ground out from under the separatists' feet? It seems logical, for the quiet revolution of Jean Lesage is helping to satisfy certain fundamental aspirations of the French-Canadian people. Yet under the Lesage government separatism has become a strong and growing movement. It is too soon to tell if in the end separatism will be defeated by the modernization of Quebec and adjustments in its relations with the federal government and with the other provinces. But it is significant that separatism began to show its strength just when, thanks to the Liberal victory of Jean Lesage (June 1960), the old constraints were beginning to weaken. Why had the movement known no success under the régime of Duplessis? It seems that the verbal, negative nationalism of the 'Chief' of the Union Nationale satisfied the confused aspirations of French Canadians who, despite their distrust of the 'English', still gave no thought to leaving Confederation. The separatist wave only began to swell after Duplessis's death. Currents of liberty and daring began to move in Quebec and radical solutions became acceptable. And, at least in the beginning, the new climate smiled not only on the Liberals but on separatist tendencies as well. The calls for secession became a thorn in the Liberal party's side, pushing it perhaps a little faster and a little farther than it had intended to go. It seems that, little by little, as the grievances of the French-Canadian people are removed or lessened, the appeal of separatism will be equally diminished. Yet the game is not yet won. A wavering on the part of the Quebec government, indifference or a hardening of attitudes in Ottawa, and separatism could still win a widespread audience. Thus, future developments depend largely on the decisions of the provincial and federal authorities. They also depend, in part, on the activities of the various separatist movements, their programs, and their ability to mobilize public opinion. It is necessary to examine them one by one in order to see their true strength and their weakness.

SEPARATIST MOVEMENTS. Raymond Barbeau, a professor of French at the Ecole des Hautes Etudes Commerciales in Montreal, founded the Alliance Laurentienne in 1957. It was a rightist movement from the start, having clerical tendencies and looking to such traditional solutions as corporatism. The Alliance Laurentienne wanted to educate public opinion, rather than become a political party. Its membership never exceeded three or four thousand and its appeal was largely to students. Its only outstanding personality was Barbeau himself. Five years later he dissolved the movement, suggesting its members join the Parti Républicain du Québec, which had just been founded by Marcel Chaput. His advice has not been widely followed. The Alliance Laurentienne had a fleeting life and a limited audience (its newspaper appeared only sporadically). But Barbeau wrote three books that helped popularize the separatist thesis – *J'ai choisi l'indépendance, Le Québec est-il une colonie?* and *La Libération économique du Québec.*[1] 'Quebec is a state that has been annexed, a colony of the Canadian Confederation,' he wrote. If Quebeckers were aware of this they 'would build a country worthy of the name, where they would no longer be servants, but masters, undisputed masters.' He believes the powers allotted to the federal government are too important, those of the provincial government too limited, and, moreover, that the whole basis of division has not been adhered to: 'Throughout its sorry history Confederation has been violated time and again by the federal government, which respects neither its spirit nor its laws.' The most damaging of these violations is 'the political and administrative centralization [which] dates particularly from the war of 1914'. But Barbeau allows his critique of political centralization to go somewhat astray when he accuses Ottawa of having created the CBC, 'thus directing thought and spreading . . . infamous

[1]Editions de l'Homme, Montreal.

international and pan-Canadian theories'. In fact, CBC radio and television programs in Quebec have been one of the most effective of all separatist weapons. Mr. Barbeau accuses English Canadians of 'still treating French Canadians like a defeated foe', and to support this charge, he quotes a speech made by George Drew, then Premier of Ontario, in 1936: 'It is not unsuitable to remind the French that they are a defeated people and that their rights are only rights because of the tolerance of the English element who, with all respect for the minority, must be considered the predominant race.' Raymond Barbeau also claims that Quebec's representation in the federal Parliament has done nothing but decrease since 1867. The number of Quebec members has fallen from 65 out of 181 to 75 out of 265, or from 36 per cent to 28.3 per cent. The number of senators has gone from 24 out of 72 to 24 out of 102, from 33.3 per cent to 23.5 per cent. A similar phenomenon can be seen in the highest levels of the civil service in Ottawa. Moreover, immigration clearly favours people who speak English over those who speak French, and the French-speaking community is Anglicizing itself rapidly; the percentage of Canadians who speak French is always lower than the percentage of French origin.

And so, concludes Mr. Barbeau, they tried to make French Canadians believe they were the equal of English Canadians, a 'cynical myth'. In fact, English Canadians have skilfully carried out the Machiavellian plot of Lord Durham, who explained in 1839: 'Assimilation will, no doubt, be slow, and until it has been accomplished, justice and political wisdom equally advise that, to bring French Canadians to renounce their mother tongue, no harsh measures be used. . . . But I repeat, we must begin now to change the character of the province and to pursue the goal with firmness, though with prudence.'

The tactic has been well carried out by Confederation, and the conclusion is inescapable: 'Confederation is an absolute evil for the French-Canadian nation.' Quebec must 'undertake its decolonization immediately', and proclaim the independence that 'is written in the lines of its history'.

The Alliance Laurentienne was often accused of fascist tendencies, a vague and probably inaccurate term under the circumstances. In 1959, or two years after the founding of the Alliance, another separatist movement appeared, this one leaning to the left. It was the Action Socialiste pour l'Indépendance du Québec (A.S.I.Q.), founded by a self-taught man, Raoul Roy, who moved from job to job without particular success at any of them. This movement, whose ideas were never too clearly defined, recruited perhaps a few hundred members, again especially among young people. In its newspaper, *L'Action socialiste,* it published violent articles about 'the colonialists in Ottawa', the 'bourgeoisie', the clergy, and the 'capitalists'. The Cuban revolution seemed to be the movement's main inspiration, as it has been to other separatist groups as well. Various of its members were also members of the Front de Libération du Québec (F.L.Q.), the first secret separatist organization to take direct action. The A.S.I.Q. collapsed following the arrests of active F.L.Q. members.

The most serious of the separatist movements appeared in 1960: the Rassemblement pour l'Indépendance Nationale (R.I.N.), which tried to bring together all separatists, whatever their personal political tendencies. In order to propagate separatist ideas more effectively, it played down the problems that could cause conflict after the 'liberation'. It attracted such talented people as Guy Pouliot, a lawyer and former law professor at Laval University; Pierre Bourgault, a journalist; André d'Allemagne, a former translator in the federal Parliament and a publicity editor; Marc Girard, a pharmacist; Jean-Marc Léger, a journalist, whose membership was long a closely guarded secret; and Marcel Chaput, who became prominent when federal authorities fired him, claiming that he had taken time from his work without permission to attend and speak at a conference.

The Lesage government and the R.I.N. took their first steps at almost the same time. Despite everything that separates them, the two phenomena were involved in the same upheaval following the death of Duplessis and the end of the Union Nationale régime.

In the beginning the R.I.N. wanted to be an educational body devoted to independence, not a political party. It had recruited nearly 6,000 members when its dominant figure, Marcel Chaput, provoked a schism that cost the R.I.N. almost one-quarter of its members. This happened at the R.I.N. conference in December 1962, when the movement elected a new president, Guy Pouliot, to replace Mr. Chaput. The latter, taking with him some 1,500 members, decided to form the Parti Républicain du Québec (P.R.Q.), for, as he claimed, a simple 'movement' could never achieve his objectives. Yet the R.I.N., as he well knew, had just decided to become a political party itself. In 1965, under the direction of Pierre Bourgault, the R.I.N. had about 9,000 members. The P.R.Q. retained the R.I.N. program in general but, pleading political necessity, dropped several items, as, for example, the one advocating non-confessional schools. Thus the P.R.Q. moved slightly to the right. But Marcel Chaput is a much better propagandist than organizer, and the new party needed an organizer. He launched the party in a blaze of publicity and then quickly found himself out of money. So he started a hunger strike, vowing not to eat until $100,000 had been contributed to party funds. Donations were far from reaching this objective, and his dramatic gesture trailed off into the ridiculous. The incident showed the true popularity of Mr. Chaput. And perhaps it also showed the relative weakness of the separatist ideal; there were not 100,000 people in all Quebec ready to donate the one dollar that would have ended Mr. Chaput's hunger strike and shown their desire for independence.

Besides these open and strictly legal movements there was, for a time, the Front de Libération du Québec (F.L.Q.). The F.L.Q. was a clandestine revolutionary movement devoted to direct, violent action. If first appeared in March 1963, and for two months planted bombs in such federal installations as barracks, military depots, post offices, and statues. In June 1963 Westmount, an English residential district of Montreal, was awakened by the noise of explosions from sticks of dynamite placed in mail-boxes. The attacks were aimed at creating general uneasiness rather than at specific people. The resulting publicity made separatism famous, both within Quebec and across the country. While most Canadians wondered about these acts of violence, there was no panic. The violence did succeed in forcing

English Canadians to take an interest in Quebec's problem – though not always with sympathy; many decided that the disturbances were merely a confirmation of their theory that French Canadians are unstable and ineffective, decidedly unworthy of the benefits of British institutions. The only countries outside Canada to take much notice were the United States, Great Britain, France, and Belgium. The press in those countries had no illusions about the events; they were surprised that Canadians were playing the role of 'terrorists', but they could not get excited about agitators who rejected political assassination. Not the United States, who had met guerrilla action in Guatemala, in Cuba, in Vietnam, and so on; not Great Britain, who remembered the Mau Mau of Kenya; not France, who knew Hitler's occupation and the wars of Indo-China and Algeria; not Belgium, with its experience in the Congo and the violent conflicts between Flemings and Walloons. The 'bombs' of the F.L.Q. caused only one death, that of a night watchman in an army depot, and only one injury, which occurred when a sergeant dismantling a bomb had it explode in his hands.

Can we strike a balance-sheet on the F.L.Q.? The accidental death of a night watchman and the wounding of a sergeant discredited the movement in the eyes of Quebeckers, for their situation is not tragic enough to push them to the violence of despair. The F.L.Q. members were arrested, tried, sentenced, and then virtually forgotten. Western Canada woke up to ask what was going on in Quebec, but their understanding of the problems of French Canada was not increased; to attract attention to a problem is one thing, but to explain it is another and more difficult one. Threats of death addressed to certain personalities and messages sent out as 'communiqués of war' were no more effective. The highest ecclesiastical authorities, particularly Cardinal Léger, Archbishop of Montreal, condemned the recourse to violence.

Finally, the main beneficiary of the dynamite explosions was the Lesage government which the F.L.Q. thought timid at best and the lackey of Anglo-Saxon imperialism at worst. Jean Lesage could tell Ottawa that his claims were hardly excessive in the eyes of certain sectors of the Quebec population, but there was a danger he would be out-flanked, and that, in the interest of the entire country, the federal government ought to satisfy Quebec's requirements. It was not until November 1964, when the F.L.Q. was dead, that the leader of the Quebec government took a public position against separatism. Until then he had kept a skilful and valuable silence during his negotiations with the federal authorities.

Does the disappearance of the F.L.Q. mark the end of violence? An Armée de Libération du Québec (A.L.Q.) has sprung up since then, issuing several tracts and proclamations, but so far it has not taken any concrete action. The inaccurate use of certain phrases, such as 'we are colonized', initially aroused enough enthusiasm among young people that they were ready to take great risks, but such enthusiasm did not survive the test of imprisonment. If Quebec were truly colonized, it would have sent forth wave after wave of volunteers for prison and, if necessary, death. Some separatists believe it proves the opposite – that Quebec is colonized to the marrow of its bones, crushed by British domination, inert, and that the only way for it to recover its dignity is to become independent. They forget that a pre-revolutionary situation cannot be invented. It takes more than the wishes of a minority to open the way to revolution. It takes a whole host of objective, not subjective, conditions. But these 'objective conditions' in Quebec led to nothing more than the quiet revolution of Jean Lesage, which is an exaggerated way of describing a simple reorganization – a useful step and significant for the future, but in no way revolutionary.

The visit of Queen Elizabeth II to Canada in autumn 1964 gave separatist groups a chance to show French-Canadian hostility to British 'domination'. The demonstrators finally agreed to disperse after their organizers had met with the people responsible for law and order. In Quebec the Queen was greeted with empty streets. The people held themselves aloof. But the situation was ambiguous; refusal to pay homage to the Queen of England is a proud reaction, quite natural to a self-reliant people. French Canadians do not have the sentimental attachment to the British Crown of their Anglo-Saxon compatriots, and their behaviour in Quebec was a gesture of real discontent. But this does not mean that Quebeckers look to independence as the only way to satisfy their aspirations. It would take still-unknown depths of disillusionment and exasperation to push them to that.

THE HUMILIATED. Separatist movements, whether they favour legal or illegal methods, have recruited most of their members from the intellectuals, especially at the student level. Daniel Johnson, leader of the Union Nationale party, whose French-Canadian nationalism is irreproachable, tells about the reactions of some farmers when he asked their views on separatism. They replied with a series of questions: would their standard of living be lower or higher in an independent Quebec; would their various payments from the government be lower or higher?

Whether you applaud or deplore such pragmatism, this is the crucial question for most farmers and workers. An economist at the University of Montreal, André Raynauld, has put forth this argument against separatism: 'The Quebec standard of living is 28 per cent below that of Ontario, and it must be admitted that independence would mean that for an indefinite period of time the standard of living would be 50 per cent below that of Ontario,'[1] for Quebec would lose its present advantages as a member of the Canadian 'common market'.

The main weakness of such an agreement, according to another economist, lies in the jump from a precise figure of 28 per cent to an unscientific guess of 50 per cent, not supported by any known statistic. Separatist Raymond Barbeau saw this weakness clearly, and he retorted, it is not enough to say that our standard of living will drop, 'it must be proved'; more than that, if the standard of living in an independent Quebec fell to 50 per cent of that of Ontario 'it still wouldn't be any lower than that of the Maritime Provinces, and that of all the free countries of Africa, Asia, South America, and Europe. Consequently, even if Mr. Raynauld's fantasy prediction were to come true, Quebec's standard of living would be no lower than that of almost every country in the world.'[2]

[1]Speech quoted in Montreal papers of February 20, 1962.
[2]Raymond Barbeau, *La Libération économique du Québec,* Editions de l'Homme, Montreal 1963, p. 30.

But despite all his arguments, using various fiscal injustices as examples, Mr. Barbeau has not proved that independence would not mean a drop in the standard of living. He simply claims: 'An independent Quebec would have powerful weapons for maintaining or restoring its standard of living.' This argument is not good enough to convince workers and farmers; becoming masters of their own economic destiny is not enough. They want assurance that their standard of living would not join those of African and Asian countries at the bottom of the economic ladder.

On the other hand these considerations make little impression on the young students who support the separatist movements. Following the most ancient of Quebec's traditions, they want to defend, protect, and improve their language, their culture, and their intellectual vitality, rather than their material standards. The basic preoccupations of these young separatists find expression in the little reviews, and without doubt the strongest of these concerns is cultural.

Thus the poets who founded the review *Liberté 60* were in revolt primarily against an historical, social, and political environment that was perverting their language. 'My native tongue is not French, it is Franglais,' wrote Fernand Ouellette,[1] who added: 'Learning French was almost like learning a foreign language.' If this language, which their fathers and their Catholic faith have defended for generations, is today almost a foreign language, it is because they themselves feel foreign in a Canada that is so predominantly English. Many of them are now ready to abandon a faith that no longer seems a necessary part of their personality, but not their language. Language is the vehicle of their entire culture, and their culture is the affirmation of their identity in an English-speaking world. For centuries, being French-Canadian meant being Catholic and speaking French in a Protestant and English environment. The Church was the guardian of tradition, and its authoritarian way of carrying out this responsibility has perhaps contributed to its intellectual mediocrity. Young people, reacting against clericalism, can reject or forget the faith, but they cannot also reject the language, their

[1]*Liberté 60*, March-April 1964.

instrument for reconquering their culture. If they can restore the richness of the language and the vitality of the culture, they will no longer be foreigners. And they do not use the word 'foreigners' in any figurative sense. As foreigners, which a minority can often be, they want to become full citizens of an independent Quebec that will give them the homeland they have not been able to find in the entity known as Canada. By remastering their language, they cease to be foreigners; by ceasing to be foreigners, they expand their culture. With totalitarianism, which can be very tempting, they identify cultural heritage with political homeland. With one stroke national independence becomes both the means and the objective of the renaissance of an impoverished language and a weakened, humiliated culture.

Their feeling is all the more intense because they themselves have been humiliated through their language and culture. Many visitors from France, shocked at the accent and impoverished vocabulary of the French Canadian, have made their opinions known with an arrogance that left no doubt in the Canadian's mind. 'We sons of workers or white-collar workers,' writes Fernand Ouellette, 'have been particularly frustrated. Our hunger for words . . . was not satisfied. . . . Our world was reduced. We were condemned to search for words that we couldn't find. And I'm convinced that a very serious sense of insecurity is the result. It isn't just a question of concrete vocabulary, a vocabulary for external objects, but rather the means of expressing our feelings, our passions, our emotions.'

And so, should Quebec become independent, it would be the scene of a great flowering of talents: 'The day when this cultural minority, which has been tolerated in this country, becomes a nation on its own,' writes Jean-Guy Pilon, 'the day this minority is independent, our literature will take great strides forward. For the writer, like any man in any society, must feel free. And a free man can do great things.'[1]

The humiliation appears in many guises; the French Canadian does not live as well as his English compatriot who lives so close to him in Westmount, or on the other side of the Ontario border. (Whatever his language, the Canadian does not live as

[1]*Le Quartier Latin,* Montreal, February 27, 1962.

well as the American, so close and so overpowering.) At work a Quebecker must often use the language of the rich, who control the economy. But he does not think of all the things that can separate the English Canadians from the British; he sees their material riches, he envies their cultural riches, and his own feelings of inferiority are intensified. But, while the social humiliation may be bearable, the cultural humiliation is not. In the name of political power, the English imposed bilingualism on him, which has bastardized his language and his spirit. He rebels:

> The man who grows up in a bilingual milieu experiences the continual mental confusion of two languages attacking his brain [writes Fernand Ouellette]. His mental structures are weakened. The brain must first have strong, healthy structures before taking on another lingual universe. It isn't surprising that Rémy de Gourmont[1] has written that 'bilingual peoples are almost always inferior peoples.' . . . There is no coexistence in a bilingual milieu; there is only the continual aggression by the language of the majority group. . . . This continual aggression paralyses the language of the minority group. It is cut off from its creative source. It becomes defensive, far more concerned with protecting itself than with creating.

The reasoning may be tempting, but Fernand Ouellette weakens it considerably by admitting in the same article that only 23.7 per cent of French Canadians are bilingual. Yet this does not mean that Quebec peasants who live in a unilingual French-language environment therefore speak a better French. Fernand Ouellette recognizes this implicitly (though he does not draw any conclusions from it) when he writes: 'The bilingualism of his [the French-Canadian's] environment and the ignorance of his leaders were against him from infancy. Today, television can supplement, at least partly, the family circle, the school, and the society. The child hears a better French. The vocabulary is richer. More of the world is at his door.'

Separatist intellectuals persist in a common attitude; they refuse to assess how much of the degradation of the language stems from bilingualism and how much from the 'ignorance of the leaders' and the mediocre school system. Bilingualism is the

[1]*Esthétique de la Langue française,* Mercure de France, Paris, 1955, p. 49.

perfect scapegoat; the English are guilty, that's enough. This explanation allows them to avoid the cruel examination of conscience that would bring to light the narrowness of the struggle waged by generations of French Canadians. The English imposed bilingualism, but Quebeckers tolerated far too long shoddy and inadequate teaching. Confederation gave them full powers in education, yet it was not until 1965 that they made use of their sovereignty in this field to which they have attached so much importance. The French language in Quebec had paralysed and impoverished itself long before the English Canadians and Americans took control of the Quebec economy. Paris, which for so long forgot about Quebec, must bear part of the responsibility – probably more than Ottawa or Toronto. But the French language in Quebec was first mutilated by Quebeckers themselves, and the English saw what fertile ground this made for anglicization. 'For too long, our desire to live has been supplanted by our memory of having lived,' wrote Fernand Ouellette, very accurately. This obsessive faithfulness to the past meant the miracle of survival for a French-speaking community in North America. But the language of this community was degenerating. Finally, after the Second World War, Quebec newspapers and school texts were given a major overhaul. At last a leap forward, however belated. Turned in on themselves, the people of Quebec seemed satisfied to have survived. Why did the awakening not come sooner? Certain school texts in New Brunswick and Ontario, where French Canadians are in the minority and not in control of the school system, used purer language, for their authors were not afraid of old taboos and dared to use the great works of French literature, whether or not those works were on the Index. But the Catholic Church in Quebec, too sure of its rights, entrusted the teaching of the language to men who were often uneducated and untalented. In all innocence these men massacred the language. But there is more to it than that; in New Brunswick and in Ontario, where the pressure to anglicize is very strong, a hard core of French Canadians have given their young a superior education, precisely because they felt more threatened than their neighbours in Quebec. Despite bilingualism, which touches perhaps one-quarter of the population of Quebec, and despite the economic predominance of the English Canadians, French Canadians in Quebec today would speak a richer and stronger language if they had refused to entrust it to the clergy.

Radio, television, and magazines from the United States are yet other factors in anglicization; but in ten years radio, television, and a revitalized press have made a strong contribution to the improvement of the spoken language in Quebec. And the educational reforms initiated by the Lesage government must mean more progress in this field. The shrivelling of the language was not an inevitable consequence of Confederation. Purifying of the language does not necessarily entail political secession. Fernand Ouellette admits this: 'Whether they choose to live in a true federation or whether they choose independence, they [the French-Canadian people] must rethink their entire society, at every level.' Political independence for Quebec will not remove the need for educational reform: courses, texts, teacher-training. It will not remove the 'continual aggression of the language of the majority group'; turning a provincial boundary into a national boundary will not change the fact that those who speak French are a permanent minority in North America. It will not wipe out American television programs, and it will not keep the *New York Times* from being a better newspaper than *Le Devoir*.

Humiliated people, aware of their humiliation, need to place the blame outside themselves. And it is all the more appealing to fix it on someone you live with but do not know. It is the English Canadian, the 'Canadian', who must bear all responsibility. To know that someone else is guilty allows you to be innocent and at the same time to feel less humiliated. Rejecting this guilty person exorcizes shame and restores lost pride. 'We're fascinated with the "Canadian" the way the sparrow is with the cat,' writes Paul Chamberland in the review *Parti pris*.[1] To clear himself, he attributes an exaggerated and false omnipresence to the English Canadian, false because the English Canadian has not been omnipresent; the French Canadians have lived turned in on themselves. 'Their greatest success has been to impose such a constraining presence on us that we have assimilated it, and it has become part of our collective burden. . . . We have made them a

[1]*Parti pris,* Summer 1964.

living part of our own being that will surely devour the rest. Not content with playing the role of the victim (who at least retains the germs of anger and revolt) we have freed them from the most odious task of all; we have been our own hangmen.'

For the *Parti pris* staff this summary psychoanalysis is more than an alibi; it is a marvellous intellectual stimulant, whether or not it twists facts and falsifies their significance. For if Quebeckers have yielded to a 'constraining presence', it has not been that of the English Canadian. It has been to the force of the conservatives who have always dominated the life of the province. Born on Quebec soil, inspired by the cult of the Ancien Régime, countering republican France with the royalist fleur-de-lis, refusing all ideas of progress, nurtured on Charles Maurras but claiming to think for themselves – all this is authentically *québécois*. The provincial political parties placed orders above justice, governed by corruption not the public interest, opposed the most elementary union claims with brute force, refused all change as a threat to power, clung to outdated structures, and achieved the ultimate in anachronisms – twenty years of the Duplessis régime in a world swirling with new intellectual, political, and social currents. There was also a backward Church, preaching the return to the land and the virtues of the craftsman, teaching individual morality in an era of great communal movements, dominating minds with the fear of sin rather than the powerful message of the Beatitudes, incapable of founding a living spirituality in a world overwhelmed by material temptations, and, in the bargain, in charge of education while adamantly opposed to all currents of contemporary thought. It is hard to face up to this 'constraining presence', which stifled the entire atmosphere of Quebec. It is easier to reject the 'Canadian'. And if you really do want to free yourself from this 'presence', it is more comfortable to call the 'Canadian' its author. But it means denying yourself the benefit of a realistic analysis because that would mean severe self-criticism, so severe that even before trying it, many have decided it would be too debilitating. Yet false diagnosis can only lead to false remedies.

This is the path unconsciously chosen by the staff of the review *Parti pris,* in which Paul Chamberland goes on to write: 'A community whose methods and economic structures are imposed from outside is helpless before the disintegration of its own human and cultural values.' He denies any responsibility on the part of Quebeckers for the economic lag in their province, for their attachment to rural structures and organizations, for their educational system which has produced more jurists than technicians or financiers, for their inability to mobilize private savings sooner for huge projects in the public interest, for the inadequate development of their natural resources, or for leaving public services in the hands of private enterprise. Initiatives on the part of the Quebec government have been carefully fitted to the code of economic liberalism, thus leaving the door open to private capital which nine times out of ten has been foreign.

And so Paul Chamberland can conclude, 'Every French Canadian is, from the beginning, sick; sick with the sickness that is Quebec. Only a violent cathartic can pull us from this neurosis; a cathartic that will brutally expel "their" presence from our being.' Throw out the 'Canadian'; internal liberation of the French Canadian will give him back his own personality and culture, and the price is the independence of Quebec.

CIVIC SPIRIT OR NATIONALISM? The problem is perfectly clear to the separatists; whether it is the economic lag of Quebec, the corruption of the French language as spoken in Quebec, or the inadequacies of their culture, all the ills of the province flow directly from Quebec's participation in a Confederation dominated by the English-speaking element. For this evil, one remedy: national independence. A French-Canadian nation exists. It cannot survive without having a French-Canadian state. Only a nation-state can lift Quebec out of its position of colony and open its way to the future.

But this appeal to anti-colonialism, though it wins over young French Canadians, meets strong opposition from their elders and particularly from men of forty and fifty. They have seen other waves of nationalism break over Quebec, they struggled against Duplessis, and they have serious arguments against the false remedy of separatism. These men instinctively fear all variations of nationalism in which they can sniff traces of Barrès or Maurras. More than that, they know that in Quebec, as Pierre-Elliott

Trudeau wrote, 'the exponents of the French-Canadian nationalist school, despite their generosity and their courage, are, for all
practical purposes, going against progress'.[1] They find it a little
easier to refute the anti-colonialist argument of the new nationalists:

> It has been claimed that any sincere anti-colonialist, who wishes
> independence for Algeria, must also want it for Quebec [Pierre-
> Elliott Trudeau wrote in 1962]. This reasoning postulates that
> Quebec is a political dependency, which shows a serious ignorance
> of constitutional history; but even so, for that to be logical it
> must also say that every Quebec separatist must want the inde-
> pendence of the Kabyles, or, to give a more striking example, the
> independence of the twenty-five million Bengalis inside India. If
> the separatists, to defeat me, reply that they really do want Bengali
> independence, I'll ask them why stop there; Bengalis speak 90
> different languages; and then, there are Bengalis in Pakistan. All
> this makes for a lot of separations!

While separatists are content to follow the logic of their nationalism, their critics try to find its roots. 'A feeling of superiority
. . . has always characterized the attitude of English Canadians
toward French Canadians,' wrote Pierre-Elliott Trudeau.

> . . . British-Canadian nationalism thus took the political form of
> what André Laurendeau[2] has admirably christened 'the theory
> of the negro king'. In the economic field, this nationalism looks
> upon the French Canadian as an idiot, but an idiot with money
> to spend. Sometimes they push magnanimity to the point of
> putting straw men – with good Quebec names – on the boards of
> directors. These men have certain things in common: (1) they're
> never good enough or strong enough to reach the top; (2) they're
> always representative enough to curry favour with the negro king
> and flatter the tribe's vanity. And finally, in social and cultural
> matters, British-Canadian nationalism expresses itself quite simply
> as contempt; whole generations of English Canadians have lived
> in Quebec without being able to understand three sentences of
> French. When these people claim in all seriousness that their jaws
> and ears are not suitably constructed to cope with French,[3] what

[1]*Cité libre*, April 1962.
[2]Editor-in-chief of *Le Devoir* in Montreal, named co-chairman of the
Royal Commission on Bilingualism and Biculturalism in 1964.
[3]This is not just sarcasm on Trudeau's part. I personally listened to a
conversation between two English-Canadian intellectuals in a large city
in the west of Canada, in which one of them insisted that English ears are
ill-adapted for catching French sounds.

they really want you to see is that they don't wish to debase those organs and their poor little sensitivities by putting them at the service of a patois. British-Canadian nationalism inevitably engenders French-Canadian nationalism. . . . For a people defeated, occupied, leaderless, expelled from commerce and from the cities, reduced to a minority, excluded from influence in the country that they had discovered, explored, and colonized, there was little choice of the means by which they could preserve the things that made them unique. This people built up a system of security, which has preserved them but atrophied them, and has made them overvalue everything that distinguishes them from the others, and look upon any change proposed from the outside with hostility.

This dread of change, promoted by a fear of losing those things that differentiate French Canadians from their English-speaking compatriots, was pushed to absurd lengths. But it was not directed solely against suggestions 'from the outside'. For generations it has opposed any change from inside as well, be it in politics, in business, or in the Church. The structures and traditions that had allowed the 'French fact' to survive had to be kept intact. They thought that this was consolidation; in fact, it was paralysis. All the while, the outside world evolved, grew, and advanced in science, technology, industry, and the realm of thought. And so, from time to time – from 1919 to 1924, then from 1933 to 1938, and finally in 1960 – a new wave of nationalism would break over French Canadians. Having put themselves into hibernation, they did not try to build themselves a worthy place in Canada, or in the world at large. When they awoke, they pitted their nation against English-Canadian nationalism and demanded a nation-state of their own.

This is the attitude that adversaries of separatism criticize. They believe they find at the heart of French-Canadian nationalism an inferiority complex that dooms it to failure. For, either this nationalist wave will recede without achieving anything, as has so often happened in the past, thus leaving it merely a matter of emotional outpouring without practical consequence, or it will lead to the creation of a French-Canadian nation-state, thus proving that the strength and power of the English-Canadian dominator and oppressor had been greatly exaggerated. So why not challenge the English Canadian within the structure of a bi-national state, so that the French Canadian can be at home not only in Quebec, but right across to the Pacific?

All this leads Trudeau to think that 'the British Canadians have only been strong by our default. And this is true not only in Ottawa, but even in Quebec, a charnel-house where half our rights have been lost by decay and decrepitude, and the rest devoured by lack of civic spirit and the microbe of venality. Under these circumstances can you wonder that British Canadians have not wanted the country to have any French-Canadian characteristics? And why would they want to learn a language or involve themselves in a culture which we have so carefully degraded at every level of our educational system?'

Thus, the separatists take Quebec into battle on bad ground. This is what Trudeau censures above all:

> All the time and energy we have spent proclaiming our rights, invoking our spiritual mission, broadcasting our virtues, bemoaning our mishaps, denouncing our enemies, and declaring our independence – none of it has made one worker any more skilful, one civil servant any more competent, one businessman any richer, one doctor any more progressive, one bishop any more learned or one politician any less of an ignoramus.

Instead of attacking the evils that Premier Duplessis bequeathed to his successors, the separatists believe they have found the magic answer in independence. In the purest of nationalist traditions they believe that an exaltation of national pride and the winning of independence will free unsuspected energies which will remake the entire Quebec landscape. If they are leftist, they quote the example of Cuba. This is to misunderstand the situation, for it was not the rupture between Havana and Washington that breathed new vitality into the Cuban society, it was the internal reforms of the Castro government that, putting power into new hands, restored hope, dignity, and courage to those who had lost it, and so encouraged them to build new structures for their society. Washington did not accept these reforms and, in the name of anti-communism, took the lead in breaking with Havana. The separatists reverse the roles, mistaking the effect for a cause, and waste their strength in a struggle that cannot improve any of the internal weaknesses of Quebec. This diversion is in fact playing the game of the conservative forces, who hope that Quebec's social and economic structures will remain unchanged, within Confederation or without. Thus Trudeau censures the separatists for giving a nationalist struggle priority over the democratic one: 'The virtue that breeds and develops democracy is civic spirit, never nationalism.' And civic spirit, in Quebec, has had a rough time.

In his book, *Pourquoi je suis séparatiste,* already cited, Marcel Chaput writes: 'Independence is much more a matter of character than of logic. . . . More than reason, we need pride. . . . It is a dangerous aberration to hope that, by some magic, the French-Canadian people will suddenly reform, unanimously demand respect for their rights, and become anxious for the correction of their language and eager for culture and great works, without first infusing them with some exalting idea.' This 'exalting idea' is independence. And Trudeau retorts: 'As if reform, respect for rights, correction of language, culture, and great works – *all of them open to us under the present Canadian constitution* – are not themselves exalting ideals!'

It is a strong argument, for the French Canadians who have fought for justice, progress, and a true culture – and they are in the minority – are, in general, not separatists. Union leaders, political figures who have fought venality and lack of civic spirit, the most dynamic members of the clergy, these men are not separatists. This does not mean separatists are venal or lack civic spirit; however, with few exceptions, they have had no concrete experience with social or political struggle. What they have not tried to do within the actual constitution, they hope to achieve in an independent Quebec. Marcel Chaput has outlined in sixteen paragraphs[1] the economic objectives of an independent Quebec:

'In an independent Quebec,' he writes, 'economic liberation would begin at our present level and could only advance if our governments apply appropriate measures:

– Repatriate to Quebec the $2 billion given to Ottawa each year in taxes and rights. [Yet the Lesage government, without modify-

[1]*Pourquoi je suis séparatiste,* pp. 98 and 99.

ing the constitution, has negotiated fiscal agreements with Ottawa that will return several million dollars a year to Quebec; to this figure must be added the budget of several 'cost-sharing agreements' financed jointly by the federal and provincial governments, from which Quebec withdrew in 1964; similar new agreements may be reached. The total of $2 billion has certainly not been reached; but an independent Quebec would have to pay much more if it wanted to organize its own foreign representation, defence, and other services at the level now assured by Ottawa.]

– Nationalize key industries: electricity, etc. [Achieved by the Lesage government within the existing federal structure.]

– Encourage manufacturing industry.

– Channel savings into French-Canadian institutions.

– Diversify the sources of foreign capital.

– Encourage the foundation of co-operative enterprises.

– Take over undeveloped sectors of economic life.

– Strengthen mixed enterprise: state and private companies.

– Compel foreign companies to hire, at all levels, a certain proportion (to be established) of Quebec citizens and French Canadians.

– Work out an over-all plan.

– Develop a national policy in economic matters.

– Profit by the example of other peoples.

– Train businessmen, technicians, economists, engineers, and other specialists.

– Lead the people of Quebec to see the state of Quebec as their ally.

– Convince French Canadians of the necessity of state participation in the economic development of the country.

– Destroy the evil myth that French Canadians have no business sense.'

But, unfortunately for Mr. Chaput, this program has already been largely carried out, or is being carried out, in a Quebec which has not become independent, but which has elected a realistic and enterprising government. Apart from fiscal agreements and the nationalization of electricity, already mentioned, all the essential points of the economic program have been undertaken. Mainly through the Société Générale de Financement, the provincial government is developing the manufacturing industries, mobilizing private savings, attracting French or Belgian capital, creating mixed enterprise, setting up steel and automotive industries, compelling foreign companies to hire French Canadians for senior positions, calling for European technicians, sending students to Europe for necessary training, preparing an over-all economic plan, etc., and, in short, 'destroying the evil myth' that French Canadians are unable to run their own economic affairs. And all this within the framework of the federal constitution.

There is no clearer demonstration that the very idea of separation is a false remedy to a real problem, that it flows from a superficial analysis of Quebec and Canadian realities, that it is born in the spirit of men who, through youth, incompetence, and lack of character or imagination, have not tried to face concrete problems and have set out to find a magic solution that will solve these problems for them. The exaltation of nationalist sentiment cannot overcome laziness of spirit or incompetence. The schools and newspapers of an independent Quebec would be no better, the writers no more talented, the clergy no more cultured; financiers would not suddenly appear and businessmen would be no more enterprising. In fact, Quebec, despite powers limited by federal prerogatives, is modernizing its schools, its newspapers, and its teaching, while one of its citizens, Cardinal Léger, was a trail-blazer at Vatican II.

The revolution that the separatists dream of is possible in a Quebec within the Canadian Confederation. It has already begun. But by claiming that independence is a necessary prerequisite to this revolution, they postpone it and divert from it the energies they waste in a nationalist campaign. Is the wild emotion aroused by a complex situation the reason why they have not yet made realistic analyses? Or is it, for some, deliberate calculation? Pierre-Elliott Trudeau, in any case, claims that some of the separatists are in fact 'reactionaries'.

TO REFORM THE CONSTITUTION. Does rejecting separatism as a false solution imply satisfaction with the present federal structures and with the way they work? Like Trudeau, the critics of separatism oppose the formula of a nation-state for Quebec. But is the present Canada really the multi-national state they are looking for?

'It would be good,' writes Trudeau, 'if Quebec's past attitude to its minority groups were to serve as an example to the other provinces that have large French, German, Ukrainian, or other minorities within their borders.' But no constitutional document has ever guaranteed the rights of ethnic groups other than the French. Under present laws, immigrants from Germany, the Ukraine, Italy, etc., have no choice but to assimilate either to the French group or to the English. This state of affairs could certainly be revised if a real desire arose for a truly multi-national state of Canada. But for the moment, Canada is a bi-national state of French and English. Creation of a multi-national Canada would collide with the nationalism of French Canadians, who can see no solution but that of a nation-state. This nationalism has always collided with English-Canadian nationalism, which, if it did not create the nationalism of French Canadians, has at least intensified it. And so Trudeau, having demolished the separatists, can go on to write: 'But I have no illusions, British-Canadian nationalism has much to do – or rather, to undo – before a pluralist state could become a reality in Canada.'

French-Canadian partisans of a federal, bi-national Canada are forever coming up against both French-Canadian and English-Canadian nationalism. One of the most distinguished proponents of this course is Gérard Pelletier, former leader of Catholic student youth, and, as a unionist, one of the leaders of the fight against the corrupt, reactionary régime of Premier Duplessis. In 1965, he became editor-in-chief of *La Presse,* the largest French-language daily in America – and a considerably better paper since Mr. Pelletier arrived on the scene. In an article for the American magazine *Atlantic Monthly,*[1] Pelletier wrote:

> Federalism exists in Canada. No matter how much Confederation has been 'rigged against the French', as the separatists contend, or

[1] *Atlantic Monthly,* November 1964.

exploited in favor of assimilation into the majority's melting pot, Quebec still enjoys more freedom and a greater measure of political independence or self-determination, than any other colonial country one can think of. That is why there is in Quebec, besides a majority of by-standers who for the time being cling to the existing order, a group of French-Canadian federalists whose analysis of the facts is quite different from the separatists' colonial theory.

The federal system, as it works at present, has not respected all the aspirations of French Canadians. And, generally speaking, the grievances that Quebeckers present to their English-language compatriots are based on incontestable facts that call into question the nationalism of English Canadians. But these grievances could not possibly furnish the alibi for a separatist adventure. Quebeckers in the past have been incapable of making intelligent use of the sovereignty they already had to further their interests. Separatists who blame the federal system for their inabilities are demanding absolute sovereignty in all domains. Quebec, they say, must get out of its colonial position. But, replies Gérard Pelletier for the federalists, 'Contemporary Quebec is by no means in the classical condition for a nationalist revolution, and *if* there is a nationalist revolution going on in Quebec, it is not developing in the kind of conditions usually associated with such movements.' He lists the four essential points that distinguish Quebec radically from colonized or semi-colonized countries whose nationalism has been fed by the political, economic, and social situations that characterize them:

'1. We, French Canadians who live in Quebec, have full control over our educational system.' This is a sphere in which 'the central government exercises no authority at all'.

'2. We enjoy a degree of political freedom and civil liberties comparable only with those of the most advanced democracies. Even the separatist movements which openly advocate the breaking up of Confederation can promote their ideas with complete freedom, and their spokesmen can run for public office if they so desire.' And it is precisely this freedom which nullifies separatist 'terrorism', violence being the last resort only for men who are refused all other means of expression. Moreover, in the article already cited, Pierre-Elliott Trudeau goes even further, claiming that fundamental liberties, compromised on several occasions by the provincial Court of Appeal, were re-established by decisions of the Supreme Court of Canada, sitting in Ottawa.

'3. We live in a highly industrialized society. Quebec's industrialization is relatively recent and is still going on at a fairly rapid pace, although it does not yet compare with that of Ontario or the United States. But more than two-thirds of the population are already engaged in industrial or administrative work and live in urban surroundings.'

'4. We enjoy a high standard of living. The annual *per capita* income reached $1504 in Quebec in 1963, which places it well above most European countries. But one of the difficulties is that Quebec's average is $230 below the Canadian average. Highest in Canada is Ontario with $2019, and the lowest is Newfoundland with $1029.'[1]

These four points are enough to distinguish Quebec sharply from colonized or semi-colonized countries where all the active elements of the population have responded to the call of the organizers and the militants for the struggle toward national liberation. And it explains why, in Quebec, separatism has not managed to mobilize the masses.

By making 'national liberation' an objective, though it does not answer the real problems of Quebec, the separatist leaders have themselves demonstrated their inability to solve these problems. They believe they are following the path of history by modelling their attitudes on those of countries that are totally unlike Quebec. Jean-Marie Domenach, in a long article in *Esprit*[2], tries earnestly to understand them, but ends up judging them severely:

Why aren't these rebellious boys, who adapt Karl Marx and Jean-Paul Sartre to the Canadian situation, out in the working-class districts and the countryside, educating the people who need it so badly . . . ? When there is so much to do, isn't it an alibi to take refuge in an all-or-nothing position, and call for revolution before any concrete emancipation? One can understand why the staff of *Cité libre,* who fought the stranglehold of Duplessism so

[1]These figures differ from those quoted on p. 134, but do not affect the argument.
[2]*Esprit*, February 1965.

courageously, sees in this an old temptation of the French Canadian: to take refuge in the security of a ready-made doctrine and in splendid isolation, a search for a 'Mother' even by those who claim to have killed her . . . , a Mother who is no longer the Church but a doctrine consisting of misunderstood fragments, a substandard abstraction that, by its radical alternatives (independence or assimilation), condemns its believers to impotence while waiting to lead them to failure.

Impotence and inevitable failure because the separatist action is based on an incorrect analysis. Federalists, such as Gérard Pelletier, thus suggest to them another view of the role of French Canadians in Canada and in North America:

Generally speaking, the federalists are no more satisfied with the present situation than the nationalists. They recognize the evidence that Confederation has failed to make Canada a bicultural country. But they do not assign the same causes to the failure, nor do they envisage the remedies in the same perspective.

They claim that French Canadians are but a very small cultural minority in North America, and they insist that, no matter what their political status may be, the situation of their group will remain a risky and dangerous one. In their opinion, the heart of the matter lies in the rapport between the five million French-speaking people and the close to two hundred million English-speaking people. For that reason, they believe that the emphasis must first be placed on the human values of the minority group itself.

To develop its culture in that kind of environment, a minority's basic need is for better education, better training, greater creativity, a better sense of reality, and the sharpest of political views. The group must be alive, articulate, vigilant, and equipped with modern techniques in every field.

Thus, despite the separatist arguments, it is not a question of despising and blaming the system and the 'English', of drawing up great lists of grievances accumulated since the death of Montcalm on the Plains of Abraham. It is a question of the relationship between the English-speaking and the French-speaking groups in North America; the relationship is disadvantageous to the French both quantitatively and qualitatively. No 'revenge of the cradle', no immigration program however massive, will modify very much their numerical inferiority. So they can, and must if they wish to survive, strengthen the 'human values' that they propose to safeguard.

This process has already begun. For, as Pelletier writes, Quebec 'has emerged from the bucolic dreams of a peasant people, isolated in its past, who resented all change and whose hope was to "survive" by fighting off all the influences from the outside world. . . . We are now less preoccupied with the necessity of defending our way of life than with the need of modernizing it. . . . Already a new vitality in the Quebec government, the presence of more competent civil servants and governmental experts among the French Canadians, and a better knowledge of public-administrative techniques have given substance to provincial projects and complaints which twenty years ago would have been mere dreams or short-lived outbursts of our collective temper.'

And, Pelletier continues, 'this process of revitalization . . . must be given priority over the dubious project of an independent Quebec. We still have a long way to go before the revamping of our society is completed. And the present constitution of Canada supplies us with enough power to go on with our house-cleaning job without interference. As we go along we might feel the need for constitutional readjustments and proceed to achieve the necessary changes, but it would be a mistake to divert our energies toward a nationalist revolution which would do very little for the social and economic advancement of our people and would in no way modify the "rapport de forces" in North America.'

Thus, while separatists reject *in toto* the federal constitution, Quebec federalists believe that it should be amended. All Quebec political parties agree about the need for constitutional reform. With the support of the Opposition, the Lesage government has set up a constitutional commission to examine the problem. Unanimity exists on one point: Quebec, the only province with a French majority, is therefore called upon to play a distinctive role in a country that claims to be founded on two cultures. Shouldn't the constitution then accord Quebec a special status within Confederation? Moreover, this special status would justify in theory what the Lesage government has been doing in practice since 1960 – placing Quebec in a situation comparable to that of no other province. Jean Lesage clearly set out this technical problem to me in November 1964:

> I was elected in June 1960 and took office on July 5. I presented our three main demands at a federal-provincial conference which began on the 25th of that same month. It is well known that we believed they would be to the advantage of the other provinces as well. We insisted on three essentials: revision of fiscal arrangements, the right of a province to opt out of certain 'cost-sharing agreements', and the repatriation of our constitution.
>
> Revision of fiscal arrangements was to give us the necessary resources for the economic programs of this province. We won agreement that the percentage of personal income tax returned to the provincial government between 1962 and 1965 be raised from 13 to 16 per cent, plus an increase of 1 per cent a year until 20 per cent is reached in 1966. We won an increase in succession duties from 50 to 75 per cent; this brought us an additional $8 million more last year. Equalization payments have been adjusted, and last year brought us another $35 million.
>
> The problem of 'cost-sharing agreements' is more complex. That is our term for some fifty programs financed jointly by Ottawa and the provinces. They cover various fields, such as social security, old age pensions, pensions for the blind and disabled, the Trans-Canada Highway, the fight against forest fires, etc. Studies on this subject have been going on for many months. In the two weeks following the Quebec conference of March 1964, Prime Minister Pearson sent the provinces his proposals for family allowances. In the case of Quebec, where we have a more advanced system, we will obtain a rebate of 3 per cent on personal income tax, which works out to $16 million. Morover, Quebec is withdrawing from twenty-nine 'cost-sharing agreements', for which we've been awarded fiscal compensation of several million dollars. I won't go into the very technical details of these different programs, each one posing a different problem. We have set up transition periods, varying from two to ten years. But in sum, we've reached our objective; we've dug out new resources for the economic development of the provinces. And I emphasize this strongly, these arrangements don't apply only to Quebec, and Quebec doesn't call for favouritism; they apply to all the provinces.
>
> That leaves the third point: repatriation of the constitution. That is, freedom for Canada to change its constitution without going to Westminster. In 1949 Ottawa asked London for an amendment to the system of dividing the seats in the House of Commons. We insisted that this amendment wait for repatriation. Whether it's a matter of division of seats, distribution of powers (from Ottawa to the provinces or vice versa), or whatever, our

concern was first to protect the provinces against any future encroachment by the federal authority, and then to negotiate with London. We won all that at the last federal-provincial conference. The constitutional commission here in Quebec is studying the question and working out its recommendations.

What will these recommendations be? Mr. Lesage defined his attitude:

We want the people of Quebec to possess the means of assuring both their economic and their cultural progress. Quebec has no intention of seceding, but we want to live in a country where bilingualism is truly respected. We reject any fusion of Quebec in a unitary whole, but we also reject complete separation. We hope to obtain, not only for Quebec but for all the provinces, agreements between the federal and provincial governments adapted to the problems of each province. In this way, we are not demanding any special treatment. Attitudes throughout Canada are in transition. We want the Canada of tomorrow to be the outcome of the common reflection of English and French Canadians and the other minorities. The diverse communities which compose the Canadian nation are destined for interdependence. They can only overcome the difficulties of their coexistence by working out freely and without restraint the path they intend to follow in the interest of all. I have cause to hope that this spirit will develop throughout the country and will lead us to a happy solution.

The intentions are clear: the Quebec government refuses pure and simple independence just as it refuses fusion in a homogeneous whole. Quebec occupies a special place in Confederation. Will this place be recognized in constitutional law as a 'special status'? That is what most Quebeckers want.

Quebec is the only province with a French-speaking Catholic majority, faithful to Roman law while the other provinces have inherited the common law of England. It asks that the amended constitution recognize its right to direct in its own way the province's schools and universities as well as various other sectors that the other provinces administer in common with Ottawa, and to work out its own methods of financing and economic expansion.

But that is not all. The provinces have no international sovereignty, and Mr. Lesage, though refusing secession, has come to claim a share of international sovereignty in certain well-defined areas, particularly in cultural matters. A first step in this direction was taken when Quebec reached an 'entente culturelle' with France in 1964. Analogous agreements – the name 'treaty' is reserved for sovereign states – could be reached with other countries either entirely or partially French-speaking. Similarly, Quebec has worked out its own contacts for the export or development of primary materials, even though the field of foreign trade is reserved to the federal authority. A constitutional amendment would make this situation official. Already the Quebec Delegation in Paris has won a special status approaching that of diplomatic recognition, even though Ottawa alone is sovereign in this field. Another example: immigration policy is reserved to the federal authorities; their policy works to the detriment of French-speaking immigrants, and thus, of Quebec. A special status could give Quebec a direct role in this field.

Thus, the situation calls on Quebec to encroach on the fields reserved to the federal power in order to solve its own problems. Ottawa and the other provinces could immobilize Quebec in a constitutional strait-jacket and halt its efforts at modernization and development. This would give separatism its golden opportunity. On the other hand, by agreeing to modify the present constitution in several areas, the other provinces would prove to Quebec that it has a place in Confederation, that its presence in the Canadian whole is more than an embarrassment or a folkloric relic, and that its presence is actively desired as a vital element in a bi-national state.

A White Paper published in Ottawa in the spring of 1965 on the repatriation of the constitution agrees that nothing in the current plans foresees 'a special status for one or another of the provinces'. Realists, however, ought to recognize that Quebec in fact is a special case that ought to be formalized by a special status so that the province can be a first-class member of the renewed federation. Refusal to do so would encourage tendencies for the complete independence of Quebec and precipitate the break-up of Confederation. This break-up would be the unfortunate consequence, not of the Quebec separatists' hazy dreams, but of the incomprehension of the English Canadians, and they would have to take full responsibility for it.

The debris, more or less patched together from what would remain of Canada, would become an easy prey for the United States, even if the innocent fiction of a pseudo-Canada politically independent but controlled economically by the United States were allowed to live on.

To avoid such an outcome, which to all intents and purposes would deprive the West of a partner indispensable to the equilibrium between the United States and Europe, English pragmatism, more than an over-concern with legal niceties, appears to be the best hope for a constructive solution. English Canadians must see Quebec's problems clearly. For, in a certain sense, the key to any solution is in their hands. What image do they themselves have of their country and its future?

IV

In Search of a Nation

'Making Canada a nation is almost an impossible task,' an English-speaking senior civil servant told me. Across the prairies, over the Rockies, right through British Columbia, the visitor meets the same question at every step, repeated twenty times over in a tone of great irritation: 'What does Quebec want? Why does Quebec want to alter the constitution?' On October 19, 1964, Ross Thatcher, Premier of Saskatchewan, remarked that 'Canada without Quebec is unthinkable', and strayed from his written text to bring up a very real danger: if Quebec were to secede, would not the English-Canadian provinces be absorbed by the United States?

Quebec, however, serenely pursues the tasks imposed on it by history and which the federal constitution has made its responsibility. In freeing itself from its obsessions, opening itself up to the outside world, and repudiating the sad legacy of Duplessis, Quebec is making its voice heard in Ottawa. And it is not just to complain and protest, but to put forward concrete proposals that can only mean new dynamism for all Canada. For if Canada wants to be a bi-national state, it cannot resign itself to the stagnation, economic lethargy, cultural atrophy, and political conservatism that have so long marked French Canada. And, even accepting the absurd hypothesis that Ottawa is carrying out a deliberate policy of assimilation, it is not in the interest of the English-speaking majority to see Quebec's natural resources poorly developed. Canada's vitality consists in the vitality of each province, and in the strength of the contacts between Ottawa and the provinces. As long as Quebec slept on, dreaming its anachronistic dreams, many private companies could make a tidy profit (fruitful investment, cheap labour supply), but the nation itself was being deprived of a good part of its wealth.

IGNORANCE AND SUSPICION. Quebec's awakening is thus considered by the other provinces as a positive contribution to the common good. Well-informed citizens cheer it on publicly. Why then is there so much fear and suspicion in some English circles? Separatist doctrines, widely publicized by the press, called up the spectre of a country torn apart. Every act of the Quebec government is examined with suspicion and, when its reasoning proves unassailable, the act is then suspect for the things it may be masking. Nobody contests the usefulness of ties between the Lesage government and General de Gaulle, but de Gaulle's opinions about 'Anglo-Saxons' are well known, and could he be using Quebec – and Canada – for some Machiavellian project of his own?

The worst thing is that most English Canadians either do not know or do not understand the claims of Quebec. In fact, they simply do not know Quebeckers themselves, or they know them but poorly. Facing the Pacific, British Columbia cares more about California and Japan than about the Gulf of St. Lawrence. Suddenly discovering that national unity is at stake, British Columbia made a gesture of goodwill and in November 1964 received the mayors of Quebec for their annual conference. On the way home the mayors were welcomed in various cities of the West. Discovering a common pioneer spirit several – though too few – Western and Quebec families arranged to exchange their children to give them a chance to learn the other language. At the same time they discovered language was not the only difference; traditions, customs, family outlook and education were also involved.

It is said that the country survives despite its geography. More than eighteen million people extend along 4,000 miles between Victoria and St. John's, Newfoundland. How can they know one another or feel that they belong to one nation? Yet geography is a weak excuse, for in Montreal itself, the two groups live side by side and still do not know each other. In the second-largest French city in the world Westmount is an English island. It is protected, not by a bristling wall, but even more effectively by language, self-satisfaction, a different standard of living, and an unbelievable lack of curiosity. This is true to such a point that recently an English-Canadian businessman remained unaware for several days that the French-language newspapers were attacking him savagely. The strange geographic configuration of the country does not explain everything, and physical proximity does not necessarily provide an opportunity to know and to understand.

French Canadians are often bilingual, but their English-speaking compatriots seldom concern themselves with learning a 'foreign' language, though it happens to be one of their two national languages. A French newspaper in Montreal decided to send free copies to the 265 members of the House of Commons in Ottawa. Two-thirds of these copies were sent back. The paper continued to mail them out. By return mail they received several dozen angry letters. 'I don't need your paper,' wrote these English-Canadian parliamentarians, 'for I don't speak French. Keep your garbage to yourselves. . . .'

Examples like this measure the gulf between the two groups. In the West, where there are very few French Canadians, English Canadians wear themselves out repeating that, if they must study another language, they would prefer to study the language of the most important minority in their province or their city. A fallacious argument, for they are not learning German, or Italian, or Chinese, or Ukrainian; and anyway, while there are more than five million French Canadians, there are only 560,000 citizens who speak German, 340,000 who speak Italian, 360,000 who speak Ukrainian, and so on. The argument reveals a provincial or local outlook that ignores a fundamental national fact: the country is first of all composed of French and English groups who together represent 86 per cent of the total population. The future of the country will be very fragile indeed until this fact is accepted.

The English-speaking traveller in Quebec can always find someone to speak to him in his own language. But the French-speaking traveller in the West feels he is in a foreign country. If he wants to spend his vacation on the shores of the Pacific, he goes to California rather than to British Columbia, for in San Francisco or Los Angeles he feels himself in a foreign country because he is in a foreign country. Thus the French Canadian knows Europe and the United States better than he knows the English-speaking provinces of his own country. Meanwhile, the citizen of Vancouver or of Calgary who travels a little, too often believes that he has understood the problems of Quebec, where in fact he has only stumbled upon the folklore. When he meets a Parisian journalist, he asks him to explain the claims of French Canada. However unqualified he may be, this improvised spokesman for Quebec discovers with surprise that his host has never taken the trouble to read the official documents that would have given him an authorized, fully documented reply, studded with facts and figures.

How can you be surprised when anger combines with juvenile spirits to explode bombs in Montreal? The situation certainly has not deteriorated to the point that violence is necessary. But the 'terrorists' helped to convince the other provinces that they should pay some attention to the problems of Quebec. Perhaps the fear aroused by those bombs is helping Mr. Lesage and his government in the work they have to do. In any case, a certain willingness to understand is beginning to appear in the West. But English newspapers give too little space to analyses of the problems of Quebec. Worse than that: as important an inquiry as the Laurendeau-Dunton Commission should have been given much greater publicity than it received from the federal government.

The progress of bilingualism is still far too slow in the federal administration, in the public service, and everywhere that it ought to be in existence. Some English Canadians from Montreal have taken up the task. They have formed bilingual groups that are debating the fundamental problems. These groups, not without a sense of humour, have chosen to call themselves *Chers ennemis*. Some English Canadians, who cannot take part in a bilingual discussion and who, faced with a menu written entirely in French, can only point to the dish chosen by their neighbour and demand 'la même chose', have formed a goodwill committee known as 'le groupe de la même chose'. This is all very touching, but larger measures than that are called for.

Meanwhile, suspicion still dominates the two camps. Jean Lesage, speaking in Toronto on November 16, 1964, avoided the two extreme solutions: 'On the one hand, the fusion of Quebec into a unitary Canadian whole, and on the other, complete separation between Quebec and the rest of Canada.' English commentators emphasized the second half, the rejection of separatism, and they showered the Quebec premier with praise. This brought on an uneasy reaction in the Lesage entourage: 'Whenever the English praise us so fulsomely, we look to see what mistake we've just made!' It is more than a joke. The distrust between the two groups amounts to an almost total lack of understanding. Language is not the only obstacle. More serious is the absence of curiosity, the profound indifference of each group to the other. They are mutually ignorant and feel no need to come out of their shells for a clear examination of the divergences that have called into question the very existence of the country. When Mr. Lesage rejects independence for Quebec, he affronts several thousand separatists; when he rejects 'the fusion of Quebec into a unitary Canadian whole', he comes up against twelve million English Canadians. By hearing the rejection of separatism and letting the other half slip by, English-Canadian journalists and politicians have merely reinforced their ignorance of the Canadian problem. And it is this ignorance that makes Quebeckers most uneasy.

For when Quebec claims a 'special status' within Confederation, when it questions the relationships of federal and provincial governments, it knows that all depends on the understanding of the English Canadians. 'A part of the Canadian people does not realize that a gulf has opened' between the two linguistic groups 'and that we have to rethink our partnership', wrote the Royal Commission on Bilingualism and Biculturalism in February of 1965. But English Canadians, occasionally encouraged by some French Canadians, do not intend to 'rethink' the country, and seem to believe that a simple 'replastering' will do. So they outline remedies that cannot meet the real problem, and only widen the gulf between the two communities.

FEDERALISM ON TRIAL. It is 'the tomb of the rights of Quebec', according to Daniel Johnson, leader of the Union Nationale. It is a 'smoke-screen masking the fundamental problems', according to the president of the Saint-Jean-Baptiste societies of Quebec. 'It' is the co-operative federalism that the Liberal government of Lester Pearson proposes to put into practice primarily to satisfy the claims of French Canada.

The co-operative federalism formula was invented by Maurice Lamontagne, Secretary of State in the Pearson government. Mr. Lamontagne admits that 'the independence essential to federalism has never been recognized by a system of consultation and co-ordination' between the different governments. Federalism has never really been carried out. That is why, now that Ottawa has decided to apply it, the authorities are trying to save its spirit by working out new protocol. Federalism being by definition co-operative, the redundancy in terms is significant. In fact, federal power clearly encroached on provincial powers until 1920 and then, after a brief period of provincial hegemony, the crisis of the 1930s and the Second World War re-established the authority of the central government.

The present phase of decentralization began in 1963 under the impetus of Quebec. The concessions made by Ottawa to the provinces have been mainly in the field of finance, concessions made to all the provinces, not just to Quebec. Then on August 15, 1964, Prime Minister Pearson informed the provincial governments that they could, if they wished, withdraw from joint federal-provincial programs. Quebec soon made use of this right.

Centralization had long favoured the English element over the French. 'Co-operative federalism', then, calls for a strictly bilingual and bicultural federal policy. The obstacles in the path of federal bilingualism are probably not insurmountable, but the effort put forward so far has been inadequate. French classes are being given to most of the ministers. Work sessions are often bilingual. In Toronto a radio station has switched from English to French, though not without arousing violent storms of protest. But compared to television, what influence has radio? French Canadians have for the first time been named to high executive positions with the Canadian National Railways, the Bank of

Canada, the Central Mortgage and Housing Corporation, the Canada Council, and various private enterprises.

But this has not solved the problem. Two societies still exist without having to communicate with each other. How can you give the French a taste for clubs and reduce the English taste for overly exclusive clubs? When nominations are made by co-optation, who can wonder that they fall to personalities like those of men already in the club, that is, to other English Canadians? How can you erase the prejudice that French Canadians are good orators and poets but incompetent economists, even when they have diplomas from the London School of Economics or Harvard? How can you attract high-quality men to Ottawa to work in an atmosphere not of confidence but of polite formality, when Quebec, since the Lesage government came to power, has such great need of talent and ability?

French Canadians who choose the federal service often find themselves caught in a cross-fire. Many English Canadians tolerate rather than welcome them, and Quebec nationalists scathe them with the epithet 'fédérastes'. Several decades of experience have convinced French-Canadian civil servants that, in Ottawa, they are second-class citizens. Some have sold out, swallowing their dignity to the point that they will perform the most humiliating tasks, such as passing reproaches on to their fellow Quebeckers that their English superiors believe will be better received if the signature at the bottom of the criticism is a French one.

'We have no place in Ottawa' is a familiar refrain in the Quebec legislature. 'We want to win out through competence,' say the young Quebeckers who have chosen to work in Ottawa. The visitor can only admire their sterling courage, and hope that English Canadians will begin to welcome them openly and equally so that Canada may survive.

A serious struggle for influence is under way between the two groups that make up the great majority of the Canadian population. A mutual desire to understand between Messrs. Pearson and Lesage has helped soften some of the rough edges. One way and another the concessions from Ottawa and the new vitality in Quebec has so far staved off disaster, that is, the break-up of Confederation.

But Mr. Pearson presides over a Liberal minority government in Ottawa (131 members out of 265) paralysed by the systematic obstruction of the official Opposition led by John Diefenbaker, the former Progressive Conservative prime minister. One revealing example was the interminable flag debate. The Liberals in their electoral campaign had promised to give the country a national flag 'that could never be confused with that of any other country'. Several suggestions built around the maple leaf were rejected by the Progressive Conservatives, who seemed to think that abandoning the Red Ensign, which carried the Union Jack in the upper left corner, would be the death knell of the country.[1]

The ties of affection and respect for Great Britain are still strong but, as Mr. Pearson pointed out when he opened the debate on the flag, they have no tinge of 'political or legal subordination'. The Conservatives, however, think that loyalty to the Crown is the country's greatest hope for survival. While Canada, fully sovereign, stands on its own feet, they still cling to a past that no longer exists. And so the English-Canadian group has its own extremists, who menace the unity of the country just as much as the Quebec separatists. This dangerous confrontation should melt into a common Canadian patriotism in which both groups could put their whole-hearted enthusiasm. For now, the extremists on both sides supply each other with arguments. The more moderate elements, caught in the cross-fire and the violence of the debate, often end up with their ideas quite thoroughly confused. The foreign visitor begins to worry when he hears highly placed leaders claiming that French Canadians are 'ashamed' of having 'sulked' through the visit of Queen Elizabeth in 1964. Nobody in Quebec is sorry that the sovereign was left to drive through empty streets.

The debate on the flag, the national symbol, gave a foretaste of the difficulties of any fundamental debate about reorganization of federal structures. The federal-provincial conference of October 14, 1964, adopted a draft bill for the repatriation of the constitution. The first step is to have it made law that the constitution can be modified in Canada, without recourse to London.

[1] The Red Ensign is the flag of the British merchant marine. It was never approved by the Canadian Parliament as a national emblem.

This would follow the British North America Act (1867) and the Statute of Westminster (1931), and be the final cap on Canadian sovereignty. The problem has been under study for fourteen years. The many texts that make up the constitution of Canada could be fused into one new text and eventually modified. Delegation of powers could be worked out between the federal and the provincial governments. But above all, they could build a country and a state where two languages and two cultures would be treated on an equal footing. By producing the 'co-operative federalism' formula, the Ottawa government has implicitly recognized that federalism has not really been in force, and has begun to make concessions, though none of them affect the constitutional structures that tie Quebec to the federal power. A second, similar, step should be taken toward satisfying the aspirations of Quebec. And here we meet the main difficulty, for it calls into conflict the two concepts of Canadian democracy.

Canada, say the French Canadians, is composed of two main groups each of whom makes its unique contribution to the common good. Members of these two groups should feel at home from Atlantic to Pacific. From Newfoundland to Vancouver Island all national institutions should be equally open to French and English Canadians. This is the price of national unity. In a true democracy the majority never ignores or restricts the rights of the minority.

French Canadians, reply their English-language fellows, have their own rights which are recognized in the province of Quebec, where they are in the majority, and in certain federal institutions. In the country as a whole and *a fortiori* outside of Quebec, they are in a minority and should not try to impose their wishes on two-thirds of the population. Democracy is majority rule. The English-speaking majority carries out its democratic responsibilities by allowing the French Canadians to administer as they wish within the boundaries of Quebec.

Quebec, then, is to be more or less a 'reserve', not unlike the reservations that exist for Indian tribes. Outside the 'reserve', the French Canadian must assimilate to the English-speaking majority. The law of majority rule does not come into play only between twelve million English Canadians and six million

French Canadians; it also works between nine English-speaking provinces and one French-speaking province. It is a game Quebec can never win. That is why it asks for a 'special status' that would make it an associate partner on an equal footing with the English-Canadian group.

'We suggest that all Canadians examine closely the concept of democracy itself,' concluded the Laurendeau-Dunton Commission. 'Too often, it has been reduced to the simple game of majority versus minority. Some English-speaking citizens before the Commission invoked the "law of the majority" as though they were brandishing a threatening weapon; some French-speaking people, who had complained bitterly of the consequences of this "law", expressed the desire to make use of it to their own advantage in a more or less independent Quebec.'

> From evidence so far accumulated [continued the Commission] it appears to us that English-speaking Canadians as a whole must come to recognize the existence of a vigorous French-speaking society within Canada, and to find out more about the aspirations, frustrations and achievements of French-speaking Canadians, in Quebec and outside it. They must come to understand what it means to be a member of a minority, or of a smaller partner-people, and to be ready to give that minority assurances which are unnecessary for a majority. More than a century ago, Sir John A. Macdonald wrote to an English-speaking friend: 'Treat them as a nation and they will act as a free people generally do – generously. Call them a faction and they become factious.' They have to face the fact that, if Canada is to continue to exist, there must be a true partnership, and that the partnership must be worked out as between equals. They must be prepared to discuss it in a forthright, open-minded way the practical implications of such a partnership. To some extent, they must be prepared to pay by way of new conditions for the future of Canada as one country, and to realize that their partner of tomorrow will be quite different from their partner of yesterday.[1]

The Commission did not overstep its terms of reference in

[1] *A Preliminary Report of the Royal Commission on Bilingualism and Biculturalism,* Queen's Printer, Ottawa 1965, pp. 137-9. The Commission is composed of Messrs. André Laurendeau (Montreal), A. Davidson Dunton (Ottawa), Clément Cormier (Moncton, New Brunswick), Royce Frith (Toronto, Ontario), Jean-Louis Gagnon (Montreal), Mrs. Gertrude M. Laing (Calgary, Alberta), Jean Marchand (Quebec), J. B. Rudnyckyj (Winnipeg, Manitoba), F. R. Scott (Montreal), Paul Wyczynski (Ottawa).

Anglicization of the French Minorities

	1951			1961		
	Total population	French origin	French mother tongue	Total population	French origin	French mother tongue
Newfoundland	361,416	9,841	2,321	457,853	17,171	3,150
Prince Edward Island	98,429	15,477	8,477	104,629	17,418	7,958
Nova Scotia	642,584	73,760	38,945	737,007	87,883	39,568
New Brunswick	515,697	197,631	185,110	597,936	232,127	210,530
Quebec	4,055,681	3,327,128	3,347,030	5,259,211	4,241,354	4,269,689
Ontario	4,597,542	477,677	341,502	6,236,092	647,941	425,302
Manitoba	776,541	66,020	54,199	921,686	83,936	60,899
Saskatchewan	831,728	51,930	36,815	925,181	59,824	36,163
Alberta	939,501	56,185	34,196	1,331,944	83,319	42,276
British Columbia	1,165,210	41,919	19,366	1,629,082	66,970	26,179
Yukon	9,096	645	308	14,628	991	443
North West Territories	10,279	954	581	14,895	1,412	994

A Canadian whose paternal ancestor settling in Canada was French, is considered of 'French origin'. The 'mother tongue' is 'the first language learned by the person, as long as the person still understands it'. Thus people can fit this category who are very Anglicized and who, for example, send their children to English schools. The above figures therefore give only an approximate idea of the real extent of Anglicization.

reaching such conclusions. The mandate from the federal government asked the Commission to study the means by which Canadian Confederation could develop *on the basis of an equal partnership between the two founding races.*

Historically, federalism has not respected this principle. Politically the 'co-operative federalism' outlined by Maurice Lamontagne and the Pearson government has not defined the structures that are to assure complete equality between the two linguistic groups. Only a federal system, however, could democratically establish this equality. If French Canadians are suspicious, it is because the federalism they have known has never been able to maintain the necessary equilibrium between one French-speaking province and the nine English-speaking ones. More than that, it has systematically violated the rights of the French minorities in the provinces with an English majority. For French Canadians, these are two serious blows – perhaps fatal ones – against the very principle of federalism.

MINORITY RIGHTS. About one million French Canadians live outside Quebec. Their situation is always a difficult one. The fate they have been accorded is one of the two principal accusations brought against the present federal system. In Ottawa a member of the Privy Council recognized that federalism has not worked out, partly because centralism has too often won out over provincial autonomy, and partly because minority rights have not been respected.

Despite centralism, French language and culture have survived in Quebec, and if they have not bloomed more richly Quebeckers can blame nobody but themselves; the province is sovereign in education. It is up to Quebec, and only Quebec, to modernize its educational structures and programs, to open them up to the realities of the world. That is why the reform of the educational system now under way is one of the most important achievements for the future.

But the position of the French minority in the English-speaking provinces is often catastrophic. Convincing proof can be found by comparing, on the decennial census tables, the number of Canadians of French origin and the number of French-speaking

Canadians (see page 122). The number of French-speaking Canadians is constantly shrinking. Separatists can justifiably claim that 'Confederation is the tomb of minorities'.[1] The rules of federalism and the principles of the constitution have not been respected, and it is glaringly obvious that the great majority of English Canadians do not wish to admit that this is the case. It is a very short step from this situation to accusations of bad faith. Even a renewed federalism will never be accepted by French Canadians as long as the injustices remain for French minorities in the English-language provinces.

Since education comes under provincial jurisdiction and the French-Canadian minorities are very unequally divided across the country, local situations vary considerably, but a few examples will suffice to illustrate the problem.

Louis Riel, the son of a French father and an Indian mother, is one of the most controversial figures in Canadian history. Riel organized the revolt of the Métis in Manitoba in 1870 and in Saskatchewan in 1885. Hanged in 1885, he has endured as a traitor to one group and as a hero and martyr to the other. Whatever else he may have been, Louis Riel was one of the principal authors of the Manitoba Act, an integral part of the constitution. This text unequivocally guarantees the use of French and the rights of French schools in that province.

The two candidates in the provincial elections of 1888, Greenway and Martin, had both promised to respect French rights in Manitoba. Once elected as premier Greenway confiscated almost all the funds of the French schools and, supported by his former adversary Martin, he suppressed the French edition of the official *Gazette*. Several months later, in March 1890, he outlawed Catholic (and French) schools and forbade the use of French in the House as well as in the courts. In all this he had the support of Irish Catholics and the opposition of English Protestants, one of whom was loyal enough to resign from the government.

The Supreme Court of Canada nullified these measures, which it declared were in violation of the constitution. But this judg-

[1]Marcel Chaput, *op. cit.*

ment was invalidated by the Judicial Committee of the Privy Council in London, which in July 1892 ruled that the French minority, while paying Protestant school taxes, could, if it wished, support at their own expense private French-Catholic schools. French was still prohibited in the House and before the courts.

These facts are not ancient history. They are at the heart of today's burning problems. Important people in Manitoba, all the while professing a certain understanding of the problems of Quebec, still claim that the discrimination is not against French schools but against Catholic schools. No matter that the French Canadians, by tying their language and religion so closely together, have furnished some appearance of validity to this argument. Quebeckers could always turn it against the English Canadians by refusing to subsidize English Protestant schools in Quebec; this would amount to the same thing, Irish schools excepted. The Western provinces would certainly complain and the federal government would be obliged to intervene. But nobody raises his voice to protest the artifice that permits them to refuse subsidies to French schools under the pretext that they are Catholic. Moreover, if the French-speaking citizens of Manitoba were to go by the letter of the law and set up French, non-confessional schools, the provincial government would quickly move to refuse them subsidies in the name of the same principle that also forbids use of French in the House and in the courts, regardless of religious persuasion.

The French minority in Manitoba is caught in an impasse. As a result, the census of 1961 shows that one-quarter of its members – exactly 23,037 out of 83,936 – no longer recognize French as their mother tongue.

The Manitoba government holds to the decision of 1892. And Ottawa shuts its eyes to the problem, arguing that the provinces are sovereign in all educational questions. But is not Ottawa the guardian of the constitution, and has not the constitution been violated? Would the Supreme Court and the federal government in the United States allow the state governments to violate, on racial grounds, the constitutional principle of equality of all citizens? The situation is even more paradoxical in Canada, where the Supreme Court had nullified the Manitoba laws, only to see them re-established by the Judicial Committee of the Privy Council in London. This submissiveness to an old London decision adds up to a strange survival of colonialism that should irritate all Canadians who are proud to be citizens of a free country.

Moreover, this submissiveness is evidence of a general conception of the law as a body of rules that must remain inviolate, whatever the upheavals of history. This static outlook justifies a certain pessimism about the chances of adapting Canadian structures to new realities. Four years after the decision of the Judicial Committee in London against French schools in Manitoba, the Supreme Court of the United States established the legal basis for racial segregation by declaring that whites and blacks were to be 'separate but equal' (1896). American judges thus admitted that segregation and equality were compatible. It took more than half a century for them to see that racial segregation in public education worked to the detriment of the Negro; in subsidy per pupil, in teachers' salaries and thus their skills, in their educational materials, the physical state of the buildings, the number of pupils per class, and the general academic level, the Negroes were always at a disadvantage. The Supreme Court then declared that segregation was unconstitutional because it violated the fundamental principle of the equality of all citizens (1954). This was an interpretation of constitutional matter that was in itself rather vague, while the revoking of the 1892 decision in Manitoba would resuscitate constitutional matter that was perfectly clear from the start. Canada must return to its basic principles by restoring the equality of the two founding groups, and pay attention to the lessons of history, which have proved that in spite of discrimination the French of Manitoba wish to retain their language. Finally, above all, the country of the future must be built on healthy foundations; Canadian unity is not threatened because

French Canadians will no longer let themselves be treated like second-class citizens; it is threatened because English Canadians will not admit that they have treated French Canadians in this way. The future of national unity is thus in the hands of English Canada. On this particular issue all that has to be done is to recognize the rights of French schools and to subsidize them just as English schools are subsidized. It would not be a revolutionary decision. It would only re-establish the integrity of the Manitoba Act. Unfortunately, the Supreme Court of Canada today has not the courage of yesterday, when it denounced the violation of the Act and only yielded when London forced the issue. The House of Commons, also having an English-Canadian majority, is no braver. But such an act of courage by Canada's leaders is badly needed as a sign that they want to preserve the national unity of which they are the guardians.

The situation in Saskatchewan was similar to that in Manitoba until the autumn of 1964, when the provincial government finally decided to subsidize French schools. But that was a political decision, and the constitutional principle has not been restored. Only restoration of that principle will allow French Canadians to have confidence in a federal system.

The trap is more subtle in Ontario, where there are 647,000 Canadians of French origin (only 425,000 of whom still speak the language). Between 1951 and 1961 the educational system has reduced the French-speaking population from 7.43 per cent of the total population to 6.82 per cent.

Yet it was an Ontarian, Sir John A. Macdonald, first Prime Minister of Canada, who proclaimed that free use of the French language would be 'one of the basic principles of Confederation'.

Today the leader of the Progressive Conservative party, John Diefenbaker, affirms that 'recognition of both the French and the English languages and cultures is the very foundation of Confederation.' And the Liberal party of Lester Pearson declares that 'French-speaking Canadians are not a minority endowed with special rights in one single province [Quebec].' These rights being valid for the entire country, the Liberal government, in virtue of article 133 of the British North America Act, 'will work resolutely for the adoption of truly effective measures so that the idea of an equal partnership will be realized, without which Confederation cannot function in an equitable and efficient manner.'

After these principles, let us look at the facts. At the present time 7,426 young Franco-Ontarians are enrolled in kindergartens where French is the main language but where they learn a little English as well. From there they proceed to primary school (eight years) which may be public (English), separate (so-called bilingual), or private (French Catholic). In 1963, 89,051 French-speaking students were enrolled in public or separate primary schools – 1,102 more than in the preceding year. In the case of separate schools (bilingual), the most favourable to the French language, the proportion of education given in English mounts progressively until it reaches 50 per cent in grade eight.

Why? Because this education leads into a secondary cycle of five years (corresponding to the American high school) where all subjects are taught in English. The French course alone is taught in French. This system is the very negation of bilingualism. Whether the student is enrolled in one of the fifty-two private schools or in one of the thirty separate schools, he will have to pass his examinations in English.

A subtle distinction further aggravates the fate of the French-speaking students. At the end of the secondary cycle, he can choose to write an 'examen de français' or a French examination. The latter is much simpler, since it is officially designed for English-speaking students who have learned the rudiments of French. Everything reinforces the French-Canadian student's impression that French is a second language. French is on a par with German or Russian. This system is so absurd that the public schools now lack enough personnel to teach French to English children.

The French minority of Ontario has organized itself as well as it can in an effort to preserve its language. L'Association des Enseignants Franco-Ontariens, 3,200-strong, stubbornly prepares education manuals, watches over the standards of its members, fights every way it can in the hope of winning respect for bilingualism.

But the situation is much more difficult in provinces where the population is numerically much smaller, even if, as in the case of New Brunswick where 232,000 people are French-speaking, they represent a much higher proportion (38 per cent) of the population. Textbooks, for example, can only be published if there are enough people to buy them. And the maintenance of a language requires enough people to support newspapers, book stores, libraries, radio programs, etc.

In New Brunswick, to choose the Maritime Province where the situation looks brightest, the use of French in schools was banned in 1871, four years after Confederation. Since then, thanks to a high birth-rate, the percentage of Acadians has risen from 16 to 38.81 per cent of the total population. In 1875 people died as the militia and the French-speaking residents clashed over the schools.

These deaths paved the way for a compromise that permits more or less legal maintenance of French schools. Local school boards may tolerate the opening of schools for the French population if they receive a petition to this effect. But the provincial capital, Fredericton, still has no French-language school. Federal subsidies allot $68 per student in the English county of Charlotte but only $26 in the French county of Restigouche. Despite the MacKenzie Report in 1955, this injustice, which brings to mind the victims of Negro schools in the United States, has not been rectified.

At the university level, provincial subsidies still favour the English ($741 a head) over the French ($89).

These inequalities and the strong Anglicizing pressure they produce are not all the work of political authorities. In many cases the politicians have received invaluable help from certain members of the Catholic hierarchy. Despite the many errors it has committed, the Church in Quebec has been a powerful factor in the survival of the 'French fact', and outside Quebec ordinary priests have played the same role. However, they have often had to struggle against the Irish bishops, who apparently were more concerned with Anglicizing the French Catholics than with preaching the gospel in their tongue.[1]

Thus in 1899 the French clergy of the dioceses of Chatham and Saint John in New Brunswick, both with French majorities, could not prevent two Irish bishops from being named over them. The clergy refused to participate in the ceremonies and, as a sign of mourning, tolled the bells in every church. The first French-speaking bishop was appointed thirteen years later.

In Windsor, Ontario, a French parish, tired of receiving only Irish priests from the Irish bishop while French priests were systematically sent to English parishes, finally turned to physical action. The new Irish priest was hardly settled in his presbytery when he was called out in the middle of the night to administer the last rites to a dying man. When he arrived at the given address, he was seized by a group of parishioners, driven to the bridge that links Windsor with Detroit, and sent to hand in his resignation to the bishop. When he refused, his parishioners left him suspended over the water, swearing they would let him drop if he did not promise to leave. And so the parish received its first French-speaking priest.

Many similar examples could be quoted to show how the provincial governments and the Irish episcopacy worked together to assimilate the French minorities into the English majority. The struggle has not destroyed the 'French fact', but it has gravely weakened the confidence that French Canadians have in the very principle of federalism.

Since the federal government has no authority in education it cannot interfere with provincial school legislation. But it must demand and win respect for the rights that the constitution has accorded the French language. Quebec is the only province that has scrupulously respected the rights of its minority; the English have schools with exactly the same facilities and the same advantages as the French. The Quebec government has a moral right to demand equal treatment for French minorities elsewhere. Some people are already complaining that Quebec is using its

---

[1]The four Maritime Provinces now have eight dioceses in which four, with French majorities, have French-language bishops.

English minority as a hostage. If the federal government really wants to save the federal system, it must take the initiative; it must modify the constitution and, by negotiation with the other provinces, bring about nation-wide respect for the fundamental principle of two equal languages and cultures. Federalism will die if the rights of the French language are safe only in Quebec. The death of federalism would inevitably bring distintegration; Quebec's secession would become inevitable, and the other provinces would become easy prey for the United States. Paradoxically, though English-Canadian nationalism has awakened and nourished French-Canadian nationalism, it has not managed to create a patriotism strong enough to resist the temptations of Americanization.

A MOSAIC OF PROVINCES. If language tends to separate Quebec from the other provinces, does it follow that language tends to bind the nine English-speaking provinces together? Quebec's claims do not diminish a more general uneasiness which weighs heavily on the country as a whole. The federal government is aware of this and does not hesitate to discuss it. 'In times of economic crisis or war,' they say in Ottawa, 'the provinces turn to the federal authorities for help and safety; in times of internal prosperity and peace, the provinces demand autonomy and national ties stretch dangerously thin.'

In the provincial capitals, it is a rare person who thinks of the country as a whole. Public opinion is concerned with more immediate questions: schools, hospitals, roads, construction, etc., which come under provincial jurisdiction. Provincial politicians echo these local concerns rather than worrying about national problems. Only a strong central government could give a true national spirit to the country, but the minority government of Lester Pearson is saddled with an Opposition that hardly seems to know what it is to be constructive. Some federal ministers talk about a 'new nationalism' which is to unite the country, but there is no evidence that it really exists. When Canadians talk about 'the government' they mean the provincial government.

This attitude is partly explained by the demographic evolution of the country. During the last ten years, the population of Montreal has risen by nearly 50 per cent (from 1,471,000 to nearly 2,110,000 inhabitants). In the same period, a city such as Calgary, which did not even exist eighty years ago, has more than doubled in size (from 145,000 to 300,000). Toronto's population has risen by 50 per cent, Vancouver's by 40 per cent, Edmonton's by 96 per cent, Ottawa's by 46 per cent, Halifax's by 37 per cent, and so on. Yet in the same ten years, the total population of the country rose by only 3.6 per cent.

This urban concentration is the product of recent and intense industrialization. It has reached such proportions that municipalities face severe financial problems in providing the necessary services for their citizens. The cities look to the provincial authorities for funds; the provincial authorities are faced with increased demands for schools, industry, and general provincial development, and they turn to Ottawa for a greater share of the fiscal resources. The federal government satisfies their demands. Outside Ottawa scarcely anyone worries about whether or not the central government is holding back enough resources for its own internal and international responsibilities. Yet provincial spending amounts to more than half that of the federal government. Can a country survive when the state shrinks while provincial autonomies flourish from Atlantic to Pacific?

This obsession with local concerns and interests is a greater obstacle to the growth of Canadian identity than either the size of the land (twenty times that of France) or the lack of population.

British Columbia, cut off from the rest of the country by the Rocky Mountains, calls itself the most dynamic of the provinces. Industrial production has more than doubled in thirteen years; it supplies 60 per cent of the cut wood in Canada, its production of crude oil has risen from $2.7 million (1961) to $25.4 million (1963). *Per capita* income is 113 per cent that of the national average. With one-quarter the population of Ontario, it supplies one-fifth of Canada's exports. In minerals alone, its exports to Japan ($58 million) almost equal Canada's total exports to France. When the hydro-electric dams now under construction on the Columbia and Peace rivers are finished, its production of electricity will be higher than Ontario's and second only to that of Quebec. Giddy with its own dynamism, British Columbia looks west, where Japan is its best client, and south, where California provides capital funds and markets, but rarely to the east to the other Canadian provinces. It is a matter of geography and provincial interests. Thus, in September 1964, British Columbia signed an agreement with the United States that brought in a $254 million cheque for joint development of the Columbia River on which three large dams will be built. An additional sum of $64 million will be received when the hydro-electric systems go into operation. With its neighbour to the south British Columbia is undertaking a far larger project than would have been possible with the other Canadian provinces. In the same way, its $250-million-a-year mineral production – zinc, asbestos, silver, lead, iron, copper, nickel, molybdenum – is largely exported to the United States and to Asia. While Quebec has Arvida, British Columbia has Kitimat, one of the world's greatest centres of aluminum, almost the entire production of which is exported. Foreign markets receive some 40 per cent of its wood production, 65 per cent of its paper, 80 per cent of its mining. And after local needs are satisfied, little is left for interprovincial trade. According to the provincial government, 50 per cent of the 591,000 salaries depend on foreign exports, while the rest are derived from local sources. British Columbia could, if necessary, carry out its economic development without any contact with the other provinces. It could even get industrial products as cheaply from the United States as it does from Ontario and Quebec.

From Vancouver it takes a day to cross the Rockies by train. Beyond Banff spreads the huge plain, all the way to Lake Winnipeg. It is the bread-basket of Canada. Is it one unit? Rectilinear frontiers mark out Alberta, with a Social Credit government,[1] Saskatchewan, with a Liberal government after twenty years of 'socialism', and Manitoba, governed by the Progressive Conservative Party. Moreover, the economy of each of these three provinces is markedly different. Alberta, rich in natural gas and oil, is the leader in mining and industry. Agricultural production is only slightly lower here than in Saskatchewan where, from 1944 to 1964, a very mild 'socialism' frightened off the foreign capital

[1]See page 152 for an attempted definition of the beliefs of this party.

The Diversity of the Provinces

	Population	%	Mines	%	Agriculture	%	Industry	%	Per capita income	%
Ontario	6,236,092	34.2	913,342	32.1	931,168	29.6	11,957,330	49.3	2,011	116
Quebec	5,259,211	28.8	516,453	18.1	456,921	14.5	7,327,258	30.2	1,508	87
British Columbia	1,629,082	8.9	235,428	8.3	151,087	4.8	1,967,091	8.1	1,959	113
Alberta	1,331,944	7.3	566,502	19.9	556,927	17.7	933,826	3.8	1,751	101
Saskatchewan	925,181	5.1	237,653	8.3	684,725	21.7	344,432	1.4	1,890	109
Manitoba	921,686	5.1	158,932	5.6	255,133	8.1	769,895	3.2	1,664	96
Nova Scotia	737,007	4	61,651	2.1	45,435	1.4	375,307	1.6	1,283	74
New Brunswick	597,936	3.3	21,811	0.8	42,986	1.4	397,457	1.6	1,144	66
Newfoundland	457,953	2.5	101,858	3.6	—	—	137,224	0.6	1,023	59
Prince Edward Island	104,629	0.6	677	—	25,005	0.8	30,041	0.1	1,075	62
Yukon	14,628	0.1	13,137	0.5	—	—	—	—		
North West Territories	22,998	0.1	17,537	0.6	—	—	3,434	—		
TOTAL	18,238,247		2,844,986		3,149,387		24,243,295		1,734	

Mining, industrial, and agricultural production is indicated in thousands of dollars and in percentages of the total. Annual *per capita* income is indicated in dollars and in percentages of the national average ($1,734).

that could have permitted similar mining and industrial development. Alberta, with oil, with ranching, and with wheat, is the Texas of Canada. Authorities in neighbouring Saskatchewan told me: 'We have less oil than Alberta, but more wheat, and, above all, we have the richest potash deposit in the world. We have returned to free enterprise, and the future is ours!' In Manitoba, the Conservatives told me: 'We have less wheat, less oil, less potash, but our economy is more diversified, more stable, and can develop under better conditions.'

The three Prairie Provinces come together on only one point: when they talk about '*the East*', lumping together English Ontario and French Quebec, they are talking about the greedy provinces that between them have locked up four-fifths of Canadian industrial production. This industry could not have developed without the sheltering tariff barriers that protected it from American competition. The equipment that the Prairie farmers order from Montreal or Toronto could be obtained from across the border for less money and with lower transportation charges.

Except for this common complaint against 'the East', the three Prairie Provinces have scarcely any feeling of belonging to one geographical and economic region. Yet they do not have British Columbia's excuse of being hemmed in by the Rockies and the Pacific. Only two thin lines traced on the map separate the three and they have many similar problems. They could unite their efforts to solve them, but such action would be interpreted as an attack on their sovereignty. They provide almost half the agricultural production of the country, yet they have not worked out any co-ordination of their efforts. Though they account for only 8 per cent of the country's industrial production, each works out its own plan for industrial development. Faced with similar problems, they have not made it any easier to find a common solution by giving themselves three governments from three rival parties.

The traveller leaves the Prairies, where a sprinkling of people live mainly on agriculture, for the richest and most heavily populated of the provinces, Ontario. One-third of Canada's population lives between the Great Lakes and Hudson Bay and is responsible for half the industry of the country, 30 per cent of its mining, and 30 per cent of its agriculture. Ontario knows that it is the richest province and that without it the country's economy would founder. Annual *per capita* income is $2,011, compared with the national average of $1,734. Each year Ontario attracts over half (51 per cent) of the immigrants coming to Canada and 34 per cent of the capital investment. This assures it of a smoother and faster development, both of its population and of its economy, than any other province. Its mining production doubled from 1949 to 1963; its industrial production rose by 20 per cent between 1956 and 1963. The unemployment rate is lower (3.8 per cent in 1963) than the national average (5.5 per cent) or the American average (5.7 per cent). Two-thirds of Canada's mechanical industry is in Ontario. The province is responsible for 90 per cent of Canada's production of electrical equipment.

Ontario's leaders, more than those of the other provinces, have a truly national outlook. Toronto knows that a good part of its industrial production is sold to the agricultural provinces and that their purchasing power depends on the harvest, on large wheat sales to the U.S.S.R. and to China, on federal protection to farmers, on credit regulations from Ottawa, etc. The provincialism of British Columbia or Saskatchewan is rarely found in Ontario, either among businessmen or among politicians. 'Our economic development depends not only on the federal government and Ontario, but on co-operation with the other provinces,' says Stanley Randall, Minister of Economics and Development. 'Some provinces have set up programs to encourage their own industrial development. These efforts could make a major contribution to the economic growth of Canada, as long as the advantages of specialization and of planning according to local resources are respected, and the waste of duplicated effort is avoided. If the development plans of the various provinces are mutually conflicting, we must work out a way of harmonizing them with an eye to the national interest.'[1]

The minister added: 'The economy of Ontario is more closely tied to the Canadian market than those of the other provinces, which means that it is in Ontario's vital interest to encourage the growth of the other parts of the country. For example, the

[1]*Legislature of Ontario Debates,* April 23, 1964.

Prairie farmer is a major factor in the increased demand this year for Ontario products, for the wheat sales to the communist countries have brought him extra revenue.'

None of this means that Ontario is not proud of its distinctive characteristics and does not sometimes yield to 'provincialism'. For example, part of Ontario's trade crusade has been to open bureaus in New York, Chicago, London, Dusseldorf, and Milan. Quebec, to mention only one other province, has 'delegations' in Paris, London, and New York. There is no theoretical reason why each of the ten provinces could not open offices in three or four foreign countries, in spite of the absurd waste of effort. In fact this process has already begun, and Ontario has pushed it the farthest, even though it has a strong voice in the federal government which has representatives in all of the countries that could possibly interest that province's economy.

But Ontario is less regional than the other provinces and has a greater sense of national reality and national interests. 'There are nine separatist provinces in this country, and one federalist, Ontario,' I was told by an English-speaking businessman from Manitoba. He was exaggerating slightly, for he was not taking into account New Brunswick, Nova Scotia, Prince Edward Island, and Newfoundland, the four poorest and least populated. They account for only 10 per cent of the nation's population, and their *per capita* income is much lower than the average.[1] These four Cinderella provinces hold out their hands to Ottawa, and Ottawa plays with subsidies and sliding scales to keep them alive and in the federation. Separatism for them would be suicidal, and they intend to remain within Confederation. Yet, from the economic point of view these provinces are a liability and not an asset. Aware of their need to attract industry, they could well work for a better co-ordination of provincial efforts, but each puts out its own plans, on such a small scale that their viability is in question.

From the Atlantic to the Pacific, each province dreams of its own steel mill, its own chemical industry, its own expansion plans. How could it be otherwise when the federal constitution

[1]New Brunswick: 66 per cent; Nova Scotia: 74 per cent; P.E.I.: 62 per cent; Newfoundland: 59 per cent.

leaves to each province the full responsibility for its natural resources? The Fathers of Confederation apparently did not foresee
the modern forms of development and economic planning, or
they would have left those rights to Ottawa. While the federal
system in the United States, especially after the New Deal and
the Second World War, has seen federal intervention in the business of the country multiply, Canadian federalism has led naturally to a certain provincial dispersion.

The tendency is strong, and has a long history behind it. In
the 1920s British Columbia wanted to meet some of its needs
by imposing a tax on exports; this was thwarted by a judicial
decision in 1930 pointing out that customs duties are the exclusive preserve of the federal government. Several years later
Alberta wanted to regulate the banking system, and the courts
prevented it from doing so since such powers belong to the
federal authority. Today, British Columbia wants to establish its
own bank. The Supreme Court of Canada had to nullify an
Alberta law relating to news dissemination, a federal responsibility. When the courts decided in 1932 that broadcasting was
a federal responsibility (apropos of the CBC), they did so in the
face of opposition from Ontario and Quebec. In the same year
Quebec, supported by Ontario, vainly contested the right of the
federal government to regulate air traffic.

All the provinces are looking for technicians and highly
specialized personnel, and all are becoming interested in organiz-
ing their own immigration campaigns in order to attract the
people they need. British Columbia rather than Quebec is outstanding in this regard, for on at least six different occasions
the federal authorities have annulled B.C. initiatives in this field
because of federal priority. Yet it is Quebec that has several good
reasons for not wanting to leave it all to Ottawa: first, prospective
French-speaking immigrants are much less numerous than those
who speak English, or even German or Dutch; second, the
authorities arbitrarily reject twice as many French-speaking
applicants as English-speaking. As a result, out of a total of
2,076,919 immigrants (1946-61), 611,983, have been British
(29 per cent), 285,729 Italian, 275,065 German and Austrian
(13 per cent), 155,550 Dutch (7.5 per cent), 42,480 French

(2 per cent). It is possible that some day Quebec will react to the arbitrary decisions of immigration officials and to its own needs, and demand 'special status' in the field of immigration. This would probably be the only method by which the province could hope to match the rising demographic charts of the English provinces and obtain the skilled personnel needed for the economic plans of the province. Though the separatists have a good argument when they talk about immigration, the Lesage government has not yet made any demand of this kind. But it is significant that British Columbia, with no linguistic factor to protect, has long been trying to modify the constitutional rules about immigration.

These few examples illustrate the provincialism that prevails in Canada. 'Throughout our history, the provinces have constantly tried to encroach on federal authority,' writes an editorialist in the *Winnipeg Free Press* after long study of the matter.[1] The unconscious priority given to provincial problems is the major danger to Canadian unity today. As grave as it is, this tendency is rarely criticized by the very people who have set themselves up as guardians of federalism. They prefer to label Quebec the one and only reason for today's unrest. But Quebec's provincialism is founded on the same economic considerations as that of all the other provinces; the provincial economy must be brought up to date. And of course, this provincialism is coupled with a nationalism that becomes virulent when the French language and culture are in danger. Quebec nationalism has traditionally stressed linguistic and cultural arguments that do not exist in British Columbia or Alberta. English Canadians claim to be annoyed by it all. They forget that their nationalism nourished French Canada's; they close their eyes to the way they have violated certain principles of federalism; they wrap themselves up in their own provincial preoccupations, and accelerate the centrifugal forces that threaten to shatter the country.

The Ottawa government knows very well that Quebec is not the only province that holds to its own ways. The Lesage government knows it too, and makes skilful use of it – Lesage won

[1]'Ottawa and the Provincial Warlords – Who Will Govern Canada?' *Winnipeg Free Press,* October 1964.

Variation in Standards of Living Between the Provinces

	Average income in dollars	Newfoundland %	Prince Edward Island %	Nova Scotia %	New Brunswick %	Quebec %	Ontario %	Manitoba %	Saskatchewan %	Alberta %	British Columbia %
1926	425		57	67	64	85	114	109	102	113	121
1930	425		56	73	65	92	124	99	61	90	126
1940	432		51	77	65	86	126	91	71	91	122
1950	979	51	56	74	69	85	121	100	87	103	123
1960	1535	57	64	76	68	85	118	101	96	101	116
1963	1734	59	62	74	66	87	116	96	109	101	113

Although the average *per capita* income has more than quadrupled in the period 1926-63, the differences in standards of living from province to province have been only slightly improved, despite federal equalization payments and subsidies.

certain concessions in the fiscal negotiations because of support from the other provinces that also need the supplementary resources. But French Canadians, as ignorant as English Canadians of the rest of the country, do not know this. They are annoyed, blustering, and angry, convinced that only French Canadians want changes made in the country's structures. They do not realize that Newfoundland, poor, sparsely settled, and physically separated from the continent, is no more isolated than the Western provinces caught up in feverish development. Too much attention and effort are centred on provincial problems to allow the sense of being a Canadian to triumph. The trees are hiding the forest.

Quebeckers complain that their income is only 87 per cent of the national average, unaware that the Manitoban is equally frustrated because he has not yet reached 96 per cent. Alberta is above the national average but unsatisfied, for it is still behind Ontario. The growth of a spirit of nationalism is also hindered by the great disparity in standards of living from coast to coast. Obviously, even further tinkering with subsidies and equalization payments could not bring about a uniform standard of living. Instead, it is partly a question of preventing wasteful duplication of effort across the country and partly one of common financing of productive investments, always with the national interest and the needs of the have-not provinces in mind. It would be an illusion to think individual income could be equalized rapidly. But the country cannot survive indefinitely if these serious regional inequalities are not corrected. Harmonious efforts at the development of the different provinces could help the country to a new awareness of its unity. Unity cannot adapt itself to the present contrast between rich-cousin and poor-cousin provinces.

Quebec is 'different' mainly on the cultural level. This upsets the other provinces much more than the poverty in Newfoundland, where the inhabitants have to get along on half the average income of Ontarians. But the cultural flowering of Quebec is closely tied to its economic development. The 'French fact' would quickly have degenerated to the folklore level if Quebec had not undertaken its economic revolution in order to leave the agricultural age for the industrial, since education is largely paid for by corporation taxes. And in return, the modernization of teaching means a supply of the trained workers needed for economic expansion. For different reasons, and with less justification, economic provincialism is as strong in British Columbia as in Quebec. The frustrations of the poor provinces and the excitement of the booming provinces combine to make Canada a mosaic of provincial strongholds that a sense of national membership cannot transcend.

A NATIONAL HAEMORRHAGE. Just as each province concentrates on its own inequalities, Canada as a whole looks to its rich neighbour to the south, one richer than the richest province. French Canadians from the Maritimes or Quebec see some of their people, for economic reasons, emigrate to an English-speaking province or to the United States, just as citizens of Alberta or Ontario cross the border to Montana or Michigan.

Two figures confirm in startling fashion the fragility of 'this hazardous but enthusiastic enterprise, Canada', to borrow a phrase from Jean Lesage.[1] One hundred years after Confederation, Canadians cannot avoid the fact that in those hundred years, ten million people have immigrated to Canada while eight million Canadians have emigrated, mostly to the United States. Why this continuing haemorrhage which almost nullifies the effect of the new blood?

As far as we know, there has been no scientific study that completely explains this phenomenon. True, average income in Canada is 78 per cent of that in the United States. But that is not reason enough. After all, 87,000 American citizens are registered with the United States consulate in Calgary, attracted north by the booming oil industry. There is no lack of opportunity in Canada for qualified and enterprising people. All of the provinces are hunting for technicians, experienced specialists, and administrators. With this shortage of trained personnel there is unemployment among people lacking the appropriate skills, and for this reason accelerated training courses have been set up.

Canada would have to double or triple its work force in order to exploit fully its soil and subsoil resources. How can you explain why such a high percentage of its population has left the country?

[1]Speech in Toronto, November 16, 1964.

Could it be that these eight million emigrants, while able to live in Canada, were unable to find a reason to live there? Perhaps they did not feel an attachment to the soil, to a country with strong enough character to hold them there. A Canadian intellectual who left for England writes, 'Canada . . . gave me everything – health, money, erudition – but she failed to give me the one thing essential: a sense of identity, without which everything else is useless. . . . One cannot go on believing in a *patria* which does not exist.'[1]

His judgement is severe, too severe. English Canadians, properly speaking, are neither British nor American, just as French Canadians, as they themselves point out, are not Frenchmen from France. But are these two groups Canadian enough? Their geography is no help. Their history is still too brief to have forged ties, traditions, a way of life, or a unity of cultural values. Moreover, the way the political system operates merely reinforces regionalism. This is true for the French Canadians, whose nationalism is in large measure a reaction to their inadequate participation in the national life, a desire to assert themselves as a nation because they do not truly feel part of the country as a whole. But it is also true for the English Canadians who have made up the great majority of those eight million emigrants.

In Victoria, as in Ottawa or Montreal, there are Canadians of both linguistic groups who feel really Canadian, that is, very different from both the 'mother country' and the powerful neighbour to the south. They carry inside them a vision of a North American country linked with Europe and with the United States, but free in its own movements – original because it is founded on two cultures and the rejection of the melting-pot; open to the Commonwealth countries with whom they share old ties and to the French-speaking countries with whom they are forming new ties; accepted by newly independent countries because Canada was never a colonizer; and tolerated or respected by Communist countries because Canada is occidental without ever having become aggressive.

Canadians who look at their country in this way are still too rare. And it is hard for them to hold to this outlook, for their ties

[1]Brian Stock, the *Atlantic Monthly,* November 1964.

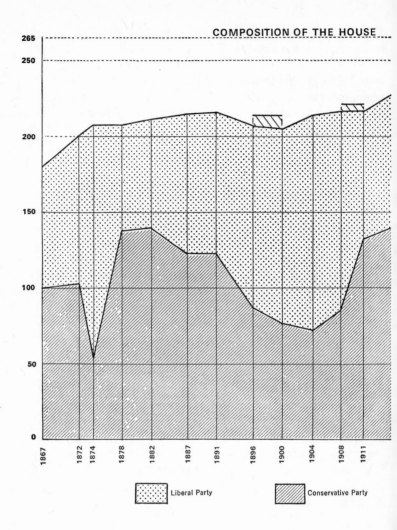

COMPOSITION OF THE HOUSE

Liberal Party   Conservative Party

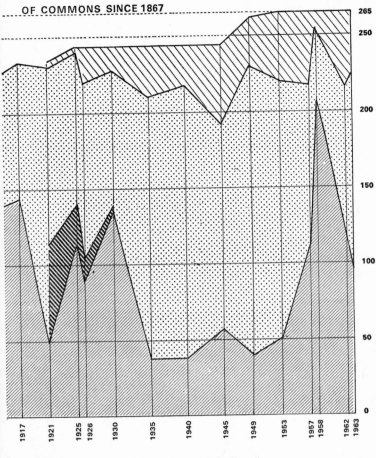

OF COMMONS SINCE 1867

265
250
200
150
100
50
0

1917
1921
1925
1926
1930
1935
1940
1945
1949
1953
1957
1958
1962
1963

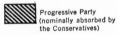
Progressive Party
(nominally absorbed by
the Conservatives)

Smaller parties:
Social Credit
Co-operative Commonwealth
   Federation — New Democratic Party
Independents

Distribution of Seats in the House of Commons since 1867

Year	Total	Majority	Conservatives	Liberals	Progressives	United Farmers	Social Credit	C.C.F.	Others
1867	181	91	101	80					
1872	200	101	103	97					
1874	206	104	73	133					
1878	»	»	137	69					
1882	210	106	139	71					
1887	215	108	123	92					
1891	»	»	123	92					
1896	213	107	89	117					7
1900	»	»	78	128					8
1904	214	108	75	139					
1908	221	111	85	133					3
1911[1]	»	»	132	86					2
1917[2]	235	118	153	82					
1921	»	»	50	117	64	11			4
1925	245	123	116	101	24	10			4
1926	»	»	91	116	13				14
1930	»	»	137	88	2				8
1935	»	»	39	171			17	7	11
1940	»	»	39	178			10	8	10
1945	»	»	67	125			13	28	12
1948	262	132	41	190			10	13	8
1953	265	133	51	170			15	23	6
1957	»	»	112	105			19	25	4
1958	»	»	208	47				8	2
1962	»	»	116	100			30	19[3]	
1963	»	»	95	129			23	17	1
1965	»	»	97	131			14[4]	21	2

[1] Plus one vacant seat.

[2] This war-time election saw the triumph of the Unionists over the Liberals of Sir Wilfrid Laurier who retained their strength only in Quebec.

[3] The C.C.F. gave way to the New Democratic Party.

[4] Including nine members of the Ralliement des Créditistes, led in Quebec by Réal Caouette.

with the Commonwealth countries are dwindling and their ties with French-speaking countries are still too feeble. At the same time, the influence of the United States continues to swell; it draws a significant proportion of the Canadian population south, and it is taking over control of important sectors of the Canadian economy. Canada has not yet managed to staunch this double haemorrhage. American companies control 95 per cent of the Canadian automotive industry, 89 per cent of the rubber industry, 64 per cent of electrical-equipment production, 50 per cent of the chemical industry, 43 per cent of paper production, 52 per cent of mineral development, and 70 per cent of natural gas and oil deposits. Foreign trade is no more diversified than foreign investments: 52 per cent of Canadian exports go to the United States and 68 per cent of its imports come from there. Nor is American influence merely economic; it is also felt in newspapers, magazines, films, etc. In the Toronto region television viewers have a choice of two Canadian and four American networks.

Canadians who worry about excessive dependence on the United States are delighted with the new dynamism of Quebec, despite its turbulence, for they see in it the possibility of a distinctive contribution to the Canadian personality. Their only fear is that the extension of provincial powers, if pushed too far, might deprive the federal government of the necessary means of asserting its authority. Such a problem may arise, but for the moment, although the definition of its powers remains intact, the federal government exercises no more authority than it should. This weakness has nothing to do with Quebec separatism. It is the result of several decades of English-Canadian provincialism degrading the two-party principle. Western Canada's tendency to spread its votes among several parties too often results in a minority government in Ottawa, constantly threatened by an Opposition coalition and unable to tackle the national problems of the country. This is a fairly recent development, dating from the 1935 election to the Commons of the first members of two English-based parties: Social Credit and the Co-operative Commonwealth Federation. The graphs and table of the division of seats in the House of Commons (pages 144-5, and 146) illustrate this trend. It should not be underestimated, for the minority parties control several Western provinces where they hold strong local positions.

Despite the occasional appearance of an Independent in the House, despite the Progressive Party, which sent 64 members to the House in 1921, the two-party system used to function effectively. Moreover, the Progressives won only two seats in 1930 and were finally absorbed by the Conservative Party, which took the new name of the Progressive Conservative Party.

In 1919 a new party, born in Ontario under the name of the United Farmers, set out on a brief career: 13 seats in 1926, 19 seats in 1930, and then oblivion.

The most durable of the minority parties are Social Credit, which sent 17 members to the House in 1935, 30 in 1962, and 23 the following year; and the Co-operative Commonwealth Federation (C.C.F.), a socialist party, which rose from 7 seats in 1935 to 28 in 1945 and 25 in 1957. Reduced to 8 seats in the following year, it re-formed itself into a new organization, the New Democratic Party (N.D.P.), which elected 19 members in 1962, 17 in 1963, and 21 in 1965.

These parties, born in English-speaking provinces, have only recently penetrated Quebec, where Réal Caouette brought in 19 of the 23 Social Credit members elected to the Commons in 1963. Shortly after, he provoked a schism; twelve members went with him to form the Ralliement des Créditistes, the others remained the Social Credit Party led by R. N. Thompson.

With the exception of this recent period, the minority parties have been the product of English Canada. The spreading of votes between the Social Credit and the C.C.F. sent minority governments to Ottawa in 1957 and 1962 (Conservative governments under John Diefenbaker), and again in 1963 (a Liberal government under Lester Pearson). This was precisely the moment when Quebec bubbled over, when a strong government in Ottawa would have been most useful for bridging the gulf that was opening once again between the two linguistic groups.

With only 112 members out of 265, the Conservative government elected in 1957 scarcely had the means to govern. Prime Minister Diefenbaker dissolved the Commons in 1958 and was returned to power with a huge majority of 208 seats, won at the expense not only of the Liberals but of the small parties of the West as well. Would he make use of this marvellous opportunity to tackle the country's problems? His international policy proved hesitant (in sharp contrast to the vigorous diplomacy of his Liberal predecessors), and his domestic policies inadequate to meet the problems of a weakened currency, a rising cost of living, and the half-million unemployed. His extremely conservative attitude left Mr. Diefenbaker unable to formulate constructive solutions.

Quebec, however, was at a turning-point; the Union Nationale was defeated in 1960 by the Liberals of Jean Lesage. Relations between the Liberals in Quebec and the Conservatives in Ottawa were very poor. The new dynamism of Quebec and the immobility of Ottawa worried the Quebec conservatives. In 1962 they elected 26 of the 30 Social Credit members, and Mr. Diefenbaker found himself again in a minority position with only 116 seats out of 265.

New elections were called for 1963. The results revealed the weakness of the Social Credit position in Quebec when the number of members elected fell from 26 to 19. The Conservatives fell (95 seats as compared to the 208 of five years before) and the Liberals rose (but only to 129 seats, still shy of a majority). The new Liberal government of Lester Pearson had to count on the support of the New Democratic Party, just as Mr. Diefenbaker had had to look to the 'Socreds'. Federal authority is weakened by all this, and paralysed in all the important debates in the Commons.

The Social Credit surge in Quebec seems to have been a passing phenomenon, for the party has not even tried to enter provincial politics there. It is the opposite in other provinces, where the Social Credit and the N.D.P. have relatively strong roots – as shown in the table of election results of 1963 (see page 150) and in the table of the composition of provincial legislatures (see page 151). The small parties have weakened federal authority by causing minority governments in Ottawa. More than that, they have weakened national cohesion by bringing to power, in the different provinces, governments with a wide variety of leanings. English Canadians have cause to worry over a weaken-

Results of the Federal Election of 1963

	Liberals	Conservatives	Social Credit	N.D.P.	Others
Ontario	1,286,791	979,359	56,276	442,340	11,896
Quebec	966,172	413,562	578,347	151,061	8,903
Nova Scotia	195,007	195,711	401	26,617	—
New Brunswick	115,036	98,462	21,050	8,899	—
Newfoundland	97,576	45,491	—	6,364	1,943
Prince Edward Island	32,073	35,965	—	1,140	—
Manitoba	134,905	169,013	28,157	66,652	826
British Columbia	237,896	172,501	97,846	222,883	4,846
Saskatchewan	100,747	224,700	16,110	76,126	443
Alberta	121,473	249,067	141,956	35,775	1,255
Yukon and North West Territories	6,114	7,783	560	—	—
	3,293,790	2,591,614	940,703	1,037,857	30,112
Distribution of seats	129	95	23	17	1

The geographic distribution of seats in the House is as follows:

Newfoundland	7	Manitoba	14
Prince Edward Island	4	Saskatchewan	17
Nova Scotia	12	Alberta	17
New Brunswick	10	British Columbia	22
Quebec	75	Yukon	1
Ontario	85	North West Territories	1

Composition of the Provincial Legislatures in 1964

	Conservative	Liberal	Social Credit	N.D.P. (C.C.F.)	Other or vacant	Total
Alberta		2	61			63
British Columbia		5	33	14		52
Manitoba	36	13	1	7		57
New Brunswick	20	32				52
Newfoundland	7	34			1	42
Nova Scotia	39	4				43
Ontario	77	22		8	1	108
Prince Edward Island	17	11			2	30
Quebec	30[1]	62			3	95
Saskatchewan	1	32		25	1	59

[1]The Union Nationale, led by Daniel Johnson.

ing of federal power; however, they should admit that they have contributed a great deal to this trend by voting for minority parties.

The small parties, with their local roots, are an offshoot of the provincialism of many English Canadians who are unable to see the country as a whole. Social Credit is based on a very vague monetary theory, and even if its theories were more concrete they would still be irrelevant at the provincial level, for the issuing of currency is entirely within federal control. It is hard to understand the surprising loyalty of several Western provinces to Socred governments. As for the C.C.F., it was in power in Saskatchewan for twenty years; during that time the population of the province remained static at 930,000, two-thirds of the university graduates moved out, and the economy lagged behind the general expansion – surprising results for a party that calls itself socialist.

But the minor parties are not the only reason for the deficiencies of the system. The federal electoral constituencies blatantly favour small rural settlements over large urban conglomerations, whose residents are the most energetic and the most open to the new ideas needed so badly by a country in crisis. Thus, the 5,656 voters in Iles-de-la-Madeleine send one member to the Commons, just like the 162,950 voters in York Scarborough (Ontario). Perhaps it is justifiable for a small island lost in the Gulf of St. Lawrence to have its own member, but this does not change the fact that there are electoral ridings having the same parliamentary weight though one has three or four times the population of the other. The problem has been recognized and a commission is now working out a redistribution that will correct the most glaring inequalities.

The progressive elimination of the minor parties and a new electoral map would put the Ottawa government on a more solid basis. This would give it the necessary authority to proceed with the vital task of bringing Canada's structures into line with its needs.

V

Building a New Canada

The resurgence of French-Canadian nationalism and the manifestations of separatism can leave no illusions: Canada is in the midst of crisis, the gravest crisis of its history, but the crisis consists of more than a conflict between the 'two founding races'. All the diatribes about bilingualism only touch one facet of a deeper sickness that affects all aspects of national life. Or more precisely, the discord between French and English reveals the unsuitability of the country's structures, the relative impotence of the authorities to meet the problems of the country as a whole. The French-English conflict, which brings into question the very bases of national unity, is certainly the most spectacular element in the Canadian crisis. But precisely because it is so visible, because it unleashes such passionate reactions, it threatens to mask the real causes of the crisis. For it is not surprising that two peoples find serious difficulty in living together in 'the bosom of a single state'. On the other hand, how could these difficulties have been so consistently ignored and misunderstood? That is the key question but the answers suggested by a study of the bilingualism crisis, in the main, go beyond bilingualism itself. They touch on the many ingredients of the mysterious alchemy that gives rise to nations.

THE STRENGTH OF BILINGUALISM. Canada is essentially the only American country that has opted for the coexistence of two different peoples within its borders, two peoples who have refused to break their ties with Europe. If its citizens cease to realize or to appreciate how unique their situation is, the existence of the country will no longer be justified and, under the pressure of its rich, melting-pot neighbour, the country will burst apart. The active coexistence of English- and French-speaking peoples could enrich the Canadian heritage, bring a new dynamism to a country that has vast potential for economic development and a vital international role. Rejection of this coexistence can only lead to paralysis or explosion.

Until now, generally speaking, the two groups have not co-existed. They are wrapped in their own preoccupations, ignoring each other, losing sight of the reasons they could have for being Canadians. English-speaking emigrants who are not eager to contribute to the growth of a country founded by two different races have no more reason to settle in Canada than in the United States, Australia, New Zealand, or South Africa. If they dream of imposing their language and their customs, they are dreaming of an achievement that after three centuries of French resistance looks pretty unlikely. Moreover, they will precipitate what could be the country's final crisis. If they are content to accept the French Canadians without being able to communicate with them, they are just as surely preparing the death of the country. French Canadians have also refused the risks and the advantages of coexistence, turning in on themselves instead of opening up to the external world and their English-language compatriots. Obviously, the victors and the vanquished of 1759 could not become partners overnight. But two centuries later the old arrogance of the one and the inferiority complex of the other are still present. Even more serious is the sum of habits acquired by the two peoples who have been either unable or unwilling to cross the gulf and discover how to coexist in the full sense of the word.

Federalism certainly seemed the only way the two groups could live together. But there has not been enough co-operation between the various governments to compensate for the partitions and divisions inherent in such a structure. The history of Canadian federalism is less the history of co-operation between federated provinces than the history of a struggle by the central government to affirm its authority and by the provincial governments to protect or enlarge their own positions. More than that, the very principles of federalism have not been respected. The clearest, the most consequence-laden example has been the violation of French minority rights in English provinces. French Cana-

Distribution of Bilingual Canadians

	Ethnic origin: British			Ethnic origin: French			Other		
	Total	Bilingual	%	Total	Bilingual	%	Total	Bilingual	%
Canada	7,996,669	318,463	3.98	5,540,346	1,665,979	30.06	4,701,232	246,730	5.24
Ontario	3,711,536	91,665	2.46	647,941	338,453	52.23	1,876,615	63,152	3.36
New Brunswick	329,940	12,096	3.66	232,127	99,158	42.71	35,869	2,241	6.24
Quebec	567,057	162,907	28.72	4,241,354	1,036,478	24.43	450,800	139,493	30.94
Montreal area	377,625	101,767	26.94	1,353,480	554,929	41.00	378,404	119,907	31.68
Other regions	189,432	61,140	32.27	2,887,874	481,549	16.67	72,396	19,586	27.05

This table, based on the 1961 census, shows clearly that in the country as a whole, French Canadians make up the bilingual portion, for only 4 per cent of the English Canadians are bilingual. But it also shows something of which few Quebeckers are aware: the percentage of bilingual people in Quebec is higher for English than for French Canadians. More than that, outside the area of metropolitan Montreal, few French-Canadian Quebeckers are bilingual, whereas one English Canadian in three, in this French milieu, is obliged to know French. The situation in New Brunswick reveals a general attitude: English Canadians are only slightly more numerous than French Canadians, but the latter group supplies most of the bilingual people – an indication of their economic inferiority.

dians have seen it as an aggression against their language, their culture, and their traditions. English Canadians have not been far-sighted enough to realize that it was an attack not only on federalism itself but on the very chances of a fruitful coexistence between the two communities. This coexistence becomes very difficult indeed if full French rights are recognized only in the province of Quebec; it would be enriched if the guarantees of the early years had not been arbitrarily broken in Manitoba, Saskatchewan, Ontario, New Brunswick, etc. Only restoration of these rights will prevent French Canadians from thinking of Quebec as their fortress and their only hope. Such negative thinking chokes off all dialogue and reduces it to an exchange of accusations and invective. Restoring the rights of the French community would not, despite the beliefs of many English Canadians, involve a 'concession' to French Canadians; it would create the necessary climate for the active coexistence Canada must have if it is to survive. To look at it as a sop to French-Canadian demands is to freeze relations between the two groups into a pattern of confrontation. To look on it as a necessary part of the co-operation between two cultures is to restore to Canada the role that justifies its existence.

It is worth while at this point to clear up the misunderstandings about the bilingual and bicultural character of Canada. Whatever their origin, many Canadians reject bilingualism, claiming it is an illusion to think of creating a country where all citizens will speak both languages. Quebeckers claim that French Canadians are almost alone in trying for bilingualism, since 30.06 per cent of the French are bilingual against 3.98 per cent of the English (see table on page 156). In their eyes bilingualism is a fraud, a weapon of progressive assimilation; English Canadians see it above all as a practical impossibility. But these two attitudes flow from a false definition of the bilingual and bicultural nature of Canada. It is not a matter of forcing all Canadians to learn both languages.[1] The essential condition is that each Canadian, within or without Quebec, should be able to take his education

---

[1]Arnold Toynbee, in an article in the *New York Herald Tribune* (July 1, 1965), suggested an impossible solution; he asked that all Canadians be bilingual.

in the language of his choice, without that choice involving any financial penalty, and that at the same time he should be able to use his native language whenever he contacts any official or public institution: federal government, Parliament, the courts, the transportation systems, etc. This sort of reform faces no insurmountable obstacle. Simultaneous translation was finally introduced into the House of Commons in 1962. Until then, French-speaking members either spoke English or spoke only to each other. A passenger on Air Canada who takes a plane to Calgary will not find one member of the staff who speaks French, but an Englishman who flies to Nice is greeted in his own language. All international airlines, driven by commercial necessity, recruit bilingual personnel. Why should it be any different inside Canada for either air or rail companies, if Canada is really a country founded by two peoples wishing to preserve their own language and culture? This concept of bilingualism, limited to official and public services, is the only one that can and should be applied. It would not prevent certain economic pressures from convincing French Canadians that they should learn English, or vice versa. Such a result would not be the ransom, but rather one of the advantages of the coexistence of two cultures. On the other hand, rejecting bilingualism in official services would be the death of coexistence.

Why did federal authorities wait until 1962 to set up simultaneous translation in the Commons? Why was the Royal Commission on Bilingualism and Biculturalism not set up until 1963? Because the English-speaking majority had lost sight of the basic character of Canadian society and, instead of seeking the contribution of French Canadians, merely tolerated them within the province of Quebec where they were allowed to live, unknown and unmolested, rather like the Iroquois on their reservations.

The crisis provoked by Quebec nationalism certainly threatens the unity, and thus the survival, of Canada. But it also gives a chance for salvation. The Laurendeau-Dunton Commission has noted the reaction of Canadians who were reminded by Quebec nationalism that the uniqueness of their country was its bicultural foundation: 'Many of those who viewed any form of union or dependence on the United States as undesirable, regarded the bicultural and bilingual nature of Canadian society as the major – if not the only – distinguishing feature which would keep Canada independent.'[1] For them, it is the only shield against the risk of 'be[ing] engulfed and drowned by the American culture'. But there will be no positive results if the only reason for satisfying French Canada's claims is to safeguard internal peace. Such an attitude leads only to token gestures: bilingual cheques, bilingual stamps, etc. These are trifling concessions, which convince French Canadians that they are wasting their time waging long and vigorous campaigns for such meagre results. If English Canadians really want to protect the Canadian identity, they will do more than calm the French Canadians by yielding on a few issues; they will take the initiative in looking for ways to affirm the bilingual and bicultural nature of their society. Reinforcing characteristics that distinguish Canada from the United States will make French Canadians feel more at home throughout the country and will deflate separatist slogans. Niggardly behaviour will only sharpen separatism; it will make no contribution to the establishment of solid bases for a Canadian identity that wishes to preserve its personality from American influences.

THE CALL OF THE NORTH. The Laurendeau-Dunton Commission also noted that some Canadians think French Canada is an absurdity on the North American continent, and that even an independent Canada is 'economically ridiculous'. Such reactions, indicative of a weakening of national spirit, are to be found on the Prairies, and also in the Maritime Provinces, whose prosperity depends to some extent on trade with the United States, and even in Quebec. The argument is always the same: Canadian well-being, through the workings of investments and commercial relations, is closely tied to that of the United States. Why bother to keep up the fiction of an independent Canada? Are not even some French Canadians ready to trade their language for increased prosperity? Summary as it is, the argument has some

[1] *A Preliminary Report of the Royal Commission on Bilingualism and Biculturalism,* Ottawa 1965, p. 56.

validity. It grotesquely overestimates the very real influence of economics on cultural life; the farmer in Saskatchewan whose prosperity depends on wheat sales to China does not feel any need to soak up Chinese culture, and 76 per cent of Quebec's French-speaking residents are not bilingual even though their economy is dominated by American and English capital. Quebeckers have risen up against the English and American companies that impose the use of English on supervisors and executives. The Lesage government has shown that it merely takes a little determination to wipe out such practices. Whether Quebec remains within Confederation or chooses independence, it will need, just as France, China, Italy, or the U.S.S.R. needs, a core of completely bilingual executives.

None the less, the desire for a better life and a greater prosperity provokes some Canadians to think of their own country as a burdensome anomaly. The fact that both English and French Canadians are tempted proves that the linguistic problem plays a secondary role in this situation. The rapid economic development of their country – the result of American support – has led many Canadians to focus their attention below the border. Inhabitants of the poorest regions, anxious to reach the North American standard of living, are most vulnerable to this attraction.

Despite all the necessary adjustments in economic, financial, and fiscal relations between the federal and provincial governments, the separatists have not managed to convince the majority of Quebeckers that Ottawa is mainly responsible for their economic lag. For one thing, the Lesage government has shown that agreement can be reached with Ottawa, and that whether in or out of Confederation, Quebec must and can work for its own economic expansion.

The federal authorities, who have allowed great regional disparity to continue, are largely responsible for the belief of some Canadians that their own country is not viable, and that annexation to the United States would be preferable. This outlook is reinforced by the closed thinking of some provincial leaders, who seem little interested in and apparently incapable of looking at their problems on a national scale. Yet there are some men who realize the great economic possibilities of their country. Why is it that these realistic men are often looked upon as dreamers?

As we crossed the Rockies under the glass dome of a Canadian Pacific lounge-car, a geology professor told me of his long winter months in the Canadian North at work with Métis and Indians on the surveying of the land, a task that is still far from complete; it was a rough but an exciting life. Week by week, the map acquired new markings, indicating a deposit of iron, petroleum, zinc, lead, nickel, uranium, coal. But young people, drawn to the comfortable city life, choose law or medicine over geology.

In Regina a mining engineer who spent fifteen years in the North spoke the same way; this land of pioneers lacks pioneers. In Ottawa a cabinet minister stated: 'Yes, our greatest resources are in the North. We don't know when they'll be developed, for we still have great reserves in areas that are already inhabited.'

British Columbia opened the way to the North when it inaugurated the Pacific Great Eastern Railway, from Vancouver to Dawson Creek, to Fort St. John, and soon to Fort St. James. Quebec is doing the same thing with its railway from Sept-Iles to the iron deposits of Schefferville in Labrador. But even these links go only a small part of the distance covered by the adventurers of seventy years ago when they rushed to the Klondike. The gold was quickly exhausted, but from the 60th parallel northward, copper, iron, nickel, zinc, uranium, etc., abound. Mining production has risen from $1,045 to $2,976 million between 1950 and 1963. Many huge deposits have yet to be explored.

This is Canada's great resource. It is also its future as a nation. To parody the words of Horace Greeley in the *New York Tribune* in 1859, one would like to tell young Canadians: 'Go North, young man!'[1] If they had already taken the risk, they would not still be asking whether or not they had a country.

But instead of turning to the North and its great potential, they head south to the easy life. In search of capital, openings and

[1]'Young man, go West and grow up with the country.' The father of this famous sentence is in fact John Babsone Lane Soul (1851).

positions, they turn to the United States, increasing their dependence on their neighbour, further diluting their own personality.

TO HARMONIZE THEIR EFFORTS. Only the federal government – or the provincial governments acting in concert – can lessen regional disparity with any degree of speed. Only the efforts of Ottawa – or the united efforts of the provincial governments – can make Canada a living, economic reality which, looking on the whole country as one huge undertaking, can appeal to dynamic and competent men, opening up new possibilities of social and cultural development and settling the question of whether or not Canada is truly a country. The provincial governments have hardly any choice; if they want to avoid seeing the federal authorities enlarging their powers to meet the task, they must unite their own efforts into one common plan. So far, they are exhausting themselves in disorganized fashion, thus wasting incredible amounts of energy and resources. Instead of reinforcing the feeling of belonging to one national whole, they encourage chauvinistic, aberrational provincialism.

Too often the provinces bid against each other for a particular enterprise, offering advantages that the less-favoured provinces cannot afford. They disperse their energies in the fields of scientific research and investment in precisely the same way. The result is unnecessary expense, duplication of effort, and unequal economic development.

In 1963 Ottawa set up an Economic Council, charged with bringing some order into this anarchy. But too many provincial officials are perfectly satisfied with this timid, and rather ineffective, gesture. The provinces seem to want to live in self-sufficiency – which is clearly impossible for any of them – ignoring the national and world contexts of their economic expansion. They have not thought of harmonizing their plans.

Federal authorities cannot interfere in a field – natural resources – assigned to provincial powers. But they could take the initiative in setting up interprovincial conferences with the aim of co-ordinating economic progress. To use a phrase still taboo in many Canadian circles, it is a question of economic planning.

Flexible economic planning would not infringe upon provincial prerogatives. Maurice Sauvé, federal Minister of Forestry, is one of the few men in public office to realize this.

Such an enterprise would counter the dominant political-economic provincialism, and give rise to a feeling of national belonging, based on concrete, vital interdependence. It would prevent the nation from becoming to a greater degree what it has already become to a lesser degree: a poorly worked-out puzzle.

The obstacles to Canadian national unity are practical ones. The effectiveness of ideological remedies is doubtful. Whatever the content of the formula, the problems will not be solved by converting public opinion to the merits of an abstract system, be it a 'co-operative federalism' or an 'associate state'. The practical difficulties must be eliminated. The anarchy of economic development is one example. Another is education: students who move from one province to another face embarrassing and annoying differences in standards. As with economic questions, interprovincial consultations in this field could mean improvements that would tighten the threads of the national fabric. There could be, perhaps not a ministry, but at least a national education service, which could help to harmonize educational programs and examinations without infringing on provincial autonomy.

To take an even more prosaic example: it is incredible that road signs are not uniform across the country. Quebec signs are a clutter of bilingualism: 'Parking-Stationnement', 'Stop-Arrêtez', etc. But Quebeckers who drive to the West meet only English: 'No right turn', 'No parking', etc. This is as it should be for the anxious guardians of French-in-Quebec-only, but it is an unnecessary annoyance for French Canadians driving across the country on the Trans-Canada Highway. The problem could be simply solved by adopting the international system used in Europe. It would be an aesthetic improvement as well. More than that, a uniform set of symbols would overcome the amazing disparity at present in use. As on the highways in France, only one word would survive: 'Stop', And that word should give the English-Canadian 'imperialists' great satisfaction.

Any strengthening of ties between the provinces would be another tangible sign that they all belong to one country; it would not limit their powers but would supply a dimension that they lack. The provinces must realize that none of them can take on the American continent. English-Canadian provincialism contributes as much as a too-narrow French-Canadian nationalism to the possibility that Canada will break up, offering the country to American hegemony on a silver platter.

Co-ordination between Ottawa and the provincial governments would give them all new dynamism. Canadians must get to know each other so that they can discover or strengthen their largely-unknown solidarity. The visitor dreams of a great welding together that will touch all the young people, of a vast program of interprovincial scholarships, of newspapers that will look beyond their own borders. Since the 'terrorists', several English-language newspapers have stationed permanent correspondents in Quebec – though this does not assure that these correspondents get to the heart of the province. But no French-language newspaper in Quebec has a permanent correspondent in Western Canada. Yet the press has an important role to play in the awakening of national feeling. Even television, excellent in many ways, shows narrow regionalism far too often; too many studies of specific problems – farming, municipalities, teaching – examine them within one province only, leaving Quebeckers ignorant of experiments in British Columbia, or vice versa. People in Montreal or Vancouver can watch what is happening in Vietnam or the Congo; these same communications media should be used to teach them about each other. They should be made aware that they all face the problem of American engulfment, or the problem of unemployment, or the need to improve economic organization.

EUROPE AND FRANCE. If Canada wants to be more than a branch office of the United States, it must diversify its foreign trade and investments. Ottawa is multiplying its approaches to the six countries of the Common Market, while Quebec is doing so more particularly towards France. But as a financial weekly in Montreal pointed out, 'the French are still hesitant about contributing to the economic growth of Quebec, while the Americans do not wait for someone to come and solicit them.'

French investments in Canada rank tenth, trailing the United States and Britain, and even such countries as Belgium, Switzerland, Holland, and Italy. Yet France has a trump to play, a card that her businessmen hardly ever exploit, though they are officially encouraged to do so. Gérard Filion, director of the Société Générale de Financement (S.G.F.), set up by the Quebec government to encourage industrialization, has some pertinent remarks on the subject. Some progress has been made after a long period of stagnation and indifference, but, Mr. Filion points out, 'Frenchmen know very little of Canada and even less of Quebec. For them, we live in a great American preserve where it would be dangerous for them to come poaching.' He deplores 'the tendency to want to control everything from Paris', and the fact that French enterprises in Canada often carry on a spirited rivalry where a certain amount of solidarity would be 'the only way to hold out against the American giants'.[1]

A former French ambassador to Canada, knowing well the potential of the country, once said bitterly, 'Imagine what the Germans would do in North America if they found six or seven million Canadians speaking their language. . . .' For French Canada is the door to the Canadian market and to the whole North American market.

Europe, and particularly France, has an important role to play in Canada, especially in Quebec. Nobody is asking French businessmen for philanthropy; they are being offered an opportunity to make a profit. By helping to develop the resources of the country, they would be helping to protect Canada from the overwhelming American influence, thus giving it greater freedom of movement and a fuller sense of its national identity. The six countries of the Common Market well understood the advantages of co-ordinating their efforts toward former African colonies. It is just as important that they work out a united policy toward Canada in the fields of foreign trade and investment. For, in the end, Europe will not be able to stand equally with the United States unless it establishes a firm base in Canada. It cannot claim that Canadian problems are of no interest, since Canada

[1]Speech of November 23, 1964, to the French Chamber of Commerce of Canada.

holds in its hands the key to the fragile economic and political equilibrium between the United States and Europe.

IDENTITY THROUGH OPPOSITION. A country is defined by more than its internal physiognomy. The other aspect is the image it projects to the world at large, the way it affirms its personality on the international scene. Canadian foreign policy could have resigned itself to being nothing but a pale reflection of American diplomacy; this would have heightened and speeded up the dependence already noted in the economic sphere. Instead, successive governments in Ottawa, and especially Liberal governments, have chosen to make their foreign policy reflect the aspirations and the outlook of Canadian society. It is a sick society that does not recognize itself in the diplomacy of its government. A country that renounces its role in the international community abdicates its personality, loses its *raison d'être,* for then it becomes entirely absorbed in internal problems that are only of academic interest to the rest of the world.

Two world wars mixed together soldiers from Chicoutimi, Saskatoon, Trois-Rivières, and Victoria in the same platoons, and carried national awareness to its highest level. After peace returned Canadians of both languages felt great pride in the diplomatic initiatives of their federal government. The government was a participant in the birth of the United Nations, and helped work out the provisions of NATO. Canada saw to the adoption of Article 2, which left the door open for a strictly military alliance to transform itself into a vast political, economic, and cultural community.

Ottawa played successful roles in great international crises, making itself acceptable as a mediator in Indo-China and in Suez. The world today is precarious, but still functioning, and part of the thanks must go to Canadian diplomacy.

The best available analyses of the 'middle-power diplomacy' have been published by John W. Holmes, Director General of the Canadian Institute of International Affairs, a former member of the External Affairs Department, and a former delegate to the United Nations. A country of eighteen million people is safe from the suspicion and defiance always visited on the Great Powers, whose strength must be feared. Thus, its very limitations become a middle power's strength, its best card. Its good offices and mediation are welcomed without fear. Whenever crisis deepens, Israelis and Arabs, Dutch and Indonesians, communists and capitalists, Laotians of whatever stripe, will all accept the help of such a country, for it can do them no harm.

The middle-power diplomacy, as long as it is active, shows the citizen of Quebec or Calgary that his country, so solidly a part of the West, cannot be lumped with the United States, or France, or Britain. The revolutionary government of Cuba, which has normal relations with Canada, knows very well that Ottawa is not Washington. But when this diplomacy seems to go into decline, the Canadian citizen, Liberal or Conservative, forgets all about it. He is hardly aware that Ottawa has been discussing recognition of Red China or membership in the Organization of American States for the last dozen years. Our role, say Canadian diplomats, is to persuade the United States without jarring it too brutally. It is an excellent principle, as long as it does not become immobility in the face of urgent problems. Canada, writes John Holmes, 'has refrained, in spite of its convictions, from embarrassing the United States by recognizing the Peking régime – although Canadian spokesmen and public opinion are growing increasingly restive.'[1] But this prudence has its limits. In Ottawa they know that abstaining from the United Nations vote on Red China, all the while selling wheat to that country, is a grave blow to the very principle of middle-power diplomacy. Is this not too high a price when Ottawa will eventually recognize Peking anyway and face the embarrassment of the United States? Otherwise, Ottawa must give up the idea of recognizing Peking, and Canadian diplomacy will sink from middle-power stature to that of a Washington echo.

The question of Canadian membership in the O.A.S. presents a similar problem. 'The difficulties in which Canada would be involved as a member [of this organization] were brought home by the O.A.S. meeting in July [1964]. If Canada had been a member, it would have had to align its policy toward Cuba with that of the United States or join Mexico in isolation, for Cana-

[1]The *Atlantic Monthly*, November 1964.

dian convictions on how to cope with Castro have been closer to those of the dissenters than to those of the United States,' writes John Holmes. But why could not Canada do as Mexico did, for both are immediate neighbours of the United States? Would a vote in the O.A.S. opposing the wishes of Washington be any more audacious than maintaining normal diplomatic and commercial relations with Cuba? Ottawa sometimes seems to underestimate its own possibilities. The American hold on the Canadian economy certainly exposes Canada to various pressures, but these pressures are limited. Washington could never push its reprisals to the point of gravely damaging the Canadian economy. Mr. Holmes has tried to explain the relative weakness of recent Canadian diplomacy:

> Some of the malaise which affects Canadians today in grasping for a useful role in world politics is nostalgia for the few years ago when they seemed to cut a more considerable figure. When a nation has the bloom of youth and has not been around long enough to step on toes, it can achieve diplomatic success which becomes progressively more difficult to get away with. Now Canada must settle down to earn respect, constructively but less prestigiously than in the past, expecting less tolerance from large and small powers, friends as well as antagonists.

What small power has shown less tolerance for Canadian initiatives? What antagonist? Only the United States balked when Ottawa convened an international conference to study the creation of a permanent peace force under U.N. control, or when Lester Pearson outlined to President Johnson his arguments against American policy in Vietnam. Cuba, the Dominican Republic, the reorganization of NATO, and the recognition of Red China are all touchy subjects between Washington and Ottawa, even though the Canadian government formulates its viewpoint with great moderation. It is tempting to reply to John Holmes that Canada, 'to earn the respect' of other nations, should affirm its positions even more clearly, rather than mute the ones that might displease Washington.

Is not the principle of middle-power diplomacy compromised when long-standing intentions dare not become actions? Paul Martin, Minister for External Affairs, seemed to admit this was the case when, during an analysis of major international problems, he said, 'We are part of a troubled world. . . . Even though we are not one of the major architects of the destiny of the world, I believe we will not shirk our responsibility to seek conditions favourable to peace between nations.'[1] But Canada's responsibility is different from that of the world's major atomic power. Ottawa will, effectively speaking, shirk its responsibilities if it aligns itself unquestioningly with Washington (despite a few speeches thrown out as proof of an independent policy).

If Canada's image on the world scene looked like a straight reflection of that of the United States, the people who read New York magazines and watch American television, work in American branch offices, and export primary materials to the south, would soon be convinced that they were in fact no different from their neighbour.

Canadians looking for their personality have an increasing tendency to think it can only be affirmed by opposing something else. Some worry about this, and with reason. Anti-Americanism, like anti-communism, should not hold a place in policy. In a thousand ways Canada is not identical with the United States; it is founded on two cultures and two peoples who preserve their identity; the United States works to melt down a multitude of races and languages in one golden pot to make one new people. Canada's federal system is evolving toward a reinforcement of provincial powers, calling for an extension of interprovincial co-operation; in the United States the central government is constantly increasing its power over the member states. With ten times the population and an infinitely larger military and economic potential, the United States is called to a role that a middle power with the greater part of its natural resources still unexploited could never fill. Canada maintains North American solidarity, yet maintains its ties with the Commonwealth and Europe as well. Only a superficial observer could ignore these fundamental differences and see only the similarities, the American Way of Life.

Do Canadians want to protect the distinctive characteristics of their country? If so, they must negotiate with each other, in order to rebuild the federal structure of their country so that a

[1]Speech, May 22, 1964.

fruitful and harmonious coexistence between the 'two founding races' becomes possible. English Canadians must repair the damage they have inflicted on the basic principle of equality between two ethnic groups. Quebeckers must accelerate the work undertaken by the Lesage government and reach out beyond their own boundaries to take in the French-speaking minorities elsewhere, for these minorities are a vital element in a society founded on two languages and two cultures. The separatists must realize that it is possible to win respect for the French-Canadian personality in Ottawa, whereas an independent Quebec would be bought at the price of much heavier subjugation to the Anglo-American environment. Secession would win Quebec a few commentaries in the Parisian press, but no support to help it assume its independence.

Centuries of misunderstanding have made this task extremely delicate and difficult. Canada must be recreated, reconstructed on more equitable foundations that will lead to new vitality. Stronger national unity is the first condition for Canadian independence from its powerful neighbour. If this unity breaks, the fragments of the country that should have been the balance between America and Europe would be gathered up by the United States. True, a united Canada can still fall further and further under the stifling influence of American capital. This is where Europe, has a role to play, not for the academic satisfaction of sustaining far-off Canadian independence, but for the very practical reason that Canadian independence is essential to European independence.

Bibliography

Aubert de la Rüe, Philippe. *Canada incertain.* Paris: Ed. du Scorpion, 1964.

Barbeau, Raymond. *La Libération économique du Québec.* Montreal: Ed. de l'Homme, 1963.

————, *Le Québec est-il une colonie?* Montreal: Ed. de l'Homme, 1962.

Bernard, Michel. *Le Québec change de visage.* Paris: Ed. Plon, 1964.

Bissonnette, Bernard. *Essais sur la Constitution du Canada.* Montreal: Ed. du Jour, 1963.

Blanchard, Raoul. *Le Canada français,* Que Sais-je? series. Paris: P.U.F., 1964.

Bruchési, Jean. *Canada, Réalités d'hier et d'aujourd'hui.* Montreal: Ed. Beauchemin, 1954.

Brunet, Michel. *Canadians et Canadiens.* Montreal: Ed. Fides, 1954.

Canada 1964. Ottawa: Queen's Printer, 1964.

Cathelin, Jean, and Gray, Gabrielle. *Révolution au Canada.* Paris: Les presses du Mail, 1963.

Chaput, Marcel. *Pourquoi je suis séparatiste.* Montreal: Ed. du Jour, 1961.

Costisella, Joseph. *Le Scandale des écoles séparées en Ontario.* Montreal: Ed. de l'Homme, 1962.

Creighton, Donald. *The Story of Canada.* Toronto: Macmillan of Canada, 1959.

Del Perugia, Paul. *Le Grand Nord.* Que Sais-je? series. Paris: P.U.F., 1951.

Dickey, John Sloan (ed.). *The United States and Canada.* Prentice Hall, 1964.

Domenach, J. M. 'Controverse sur un Nationalisme', *Esprit,* February 1965.

Dominique de Sainte-Denis, P. *L'Eglise catholique du Canada.* Montreal: Ed. Thau, 1956.

En grève, an anthology with a preface by Jean Marchand, president of the Confédération des Syndicats Nationaux. Montreal: Ed. du Jour, 1963.

Gayet, Robert Lacour. *Histoire du Canada*. Paris, 1966.

Giraud, Marcel. *Histoire du Canada*. Que Sais-je? series. Paris: P.U.F., 1961.

Johnson, Daniel. *Egalité ou indépendance*. Montreal: Ed. Renaissance, 1965.

Johnson, H. G. *Canada in a Changing World Economy*. Toronto: University of Toronto Press, 1962.

Juillard, Etienne. *L'Economie du Canada*. Que Sais-je? series. Paris: P.U.F., 1964.

Knowles, Stanley. *Le Nouveau Parti*, with a preface by Gérard Filion. Montreal: Ed. du Jour, 1961.

Le Blanc, Emery. *Les Acadiens*. Montreal: Ed. de l'Homme, 1963.

'Le Québec', special edition of *Perspectives d'Outre-mer*. Monaco: Ed. Bory, 1964.

Osler, E. B. *Louis Riel, un homme à pendre*. Translated by Rossel Vien. Montreal: Ed. du Jour, 1963.

Richardson, B. T. *Canada and Mr. Diefenbaker*. Toronto: McClelland & Stewart, 1962.

Royal Commission on Bilingualism and Biculturalism. *Preliminary Report*. Ottawa: Queen's Printer, 1965.

Sandwell, B. K. *La Nation canadienne*. Monaco: Ed. du Rocher, 1954.

Siegfried, André. *Le Canada, puissance internationale*. Paris: 1937.

Toulat, Jean. *Canada, Terre de France*. Paris: Ed. Guy Victor, 1960.

Trudeau, Pierre-Elliott (ed.). *La grève de l'amiante*. Montreal: Cité Libre, 1956.

Williams, John R. *The Conservative Party of Canada, 1920-49*. Durham, N.C.: Duke University Press, 1956.

Index